AMPLIFIERS

AMPLIFIERS

The Power of
MOTIVATIONAL LEADERSHIP
to Inspire and Influence

MATT CHURCH

WILEY

First published in 2013 by John Wiley & Sons Australia, Ltd
42 McDougall St, Milton Qld 4064

Office also in Melbourne

Typeset in 12/14.5 pt Bembo Std Regular

© Matt Church Pty Ltd

The moral rights of the author have been asserted

National Library of Australia Cataloguing-in-Publication data:

Author:	Church, Matt
Title:	Amplifiers: the power of motivational leadership to inspire and influence / Matt Church.
ISBN:	9780730304906 (pbk)
	9780730304913 (ebook)
Notes:	Includes index.
Subjects:	Leadership.
	Motivation (Psychology)
	Self-actualisation (Psychology).
	Attitude (Psychology).
Dewey Number:	658.4092

Cover design by Paul Dinovo

Cover images: © iStockphoto.com/manley099 (background); iStockphoto.com/rambo182 (amplifier)

Author photograph by James Mepham, Jungle Jim Documentary Pictures, james@junglejim.com.au

Printed in Singapore by C.O.S. Printers Pte Ltd

10 9 8 7 6 5 4 3 2

Disclaimer

The material in this publication is of the nature of general comment only, and does not represent professional advice. It is not intended to provide specific guidance for particular circumstances and it should not be relied on as the basis for any decision to take action or not take action on any matter which it covers. Readers should obtain professional advice where appropriate, before making any such decision. To the maximum extent permitted by law, the author and publisher disclaim all responsibility and liability to any person, arising directly or indirectly from any person taking or not taking action based on the information in this publication.

Contents

About the author

Matt Church is one of Australia's most enduring motivation speakers. He has been named educator of the year by the National Speakers Association and has been awarded pretty much every accolade his peers can give. He is generous with his knowledge and is the name behind many of the world's leading non-fiction business authors and professional speakers. Matt lives in Sydney, Australia and continues to write, speak and teach the art of oration through his Speakership programs for aspiring amplifiers. In 2001 he founded an international education business, Thought Leaders Global, dedicated to helping clever people be commercially smart. He is the chairman of the business and spends his time developing curriculum and inspiring great thinking and great conversations.

Acknowledgements

Gratitude is such a fabulous act. It turns your attention from the self to others. Gratitude lists are used as depression therapy in some cases and the giving of thanks is something to cherish and honour.

I would first like to thank my family for their commitment, support and understanding in putting up with me while I locked myself away in the study to write.

On a personal level I would like to thank Lex, my gorgeous wife of over 20 years. I believe that all I am professionally, and indeed the idea of amplifiers, came from Lex. The title was her idea, shared one day on a walk. As the best and brightest in the fitness industry Lex revolutionised group exercise to music. She combined science, through her masters degree and art, through her professional dance background, to take the methodology of group fitness to another level altogether—Lex was one of the first amplifiers I ever met in person.

Of course the brilliant Chloe and amazing Nicholas know that when Mum or Dad are away they are working on being amplifiers and helping to make their future world a better place, if we can. Love you guys: you make me want to be a better man.

In addition, Lucy Raymond and the team at Wiley have been so amazing to work with. I loved our meetings and am so honoured by the investment you all put into each and every project. You amplify each time you publish as you help share great ideas with the planet.

My English and grammar are atrocious and so, Wendy Church and Neville Cook, you made my words so much better. Thank you for editing the work with so much care: you were the first to read my thoughts and your attention to detail makes the journey for readers so much smoother.

I'd like to thank all the thought leaders I have worked with over the years: your ideas have shaped my thoughts as much as mine may have shaped yours. You all rock!

My business partners at Thought Leaders Global are amazing. Thank you Michael, Scott, Pete, Shar, PK, Mark, Neen, Mel, Don and Marcus. The whole focus on business as a force for change is the result of your thoughts and talents. A specific mention to Michael Henderson for his vision around leaders worth following, work worth doing and cultures worth belonging to—love your brain mate.

And finally to you as the reader. Thank you for taking the time to broaden your ideas and for bringing the idea of being an amplifier to all areas of your life.

Manifesto: it's not just talk

Leaders today need to go 'old school'—they need to get back to those original base actions of meeting, talking and inspiring the people around them. They need to get out from behind their strategy and bring leadership to life. They need to be able to make a difference personally. Their very role as leaders, the purpose of their existence, is to make a difference and the difference they make is one of *amplification*.

Great leaders need to be able to make more out of what is going on around them—they maximise what is working. Great leaders *amplify* the messages that matter; they *amplify* the commitment to getting things done; they *amplify* the positive mood in a culture; and they *amplify* the results they get. *Amplifiers* are those leaders who make a difference at all levels within a business, a community or a family.

The challenge is that being an amplifier is a choice you make, more so than a promotion you get or a set of capabilities you develop. It's the choice you make to be a motivational leader, to make a positive difference to the human condition in and around you.

A memo or a slide show are all well and good, but they are minnows when stacked alongside the whale that is motivational leadership. Motivational leadership is the ability to influence culture and drive change. It can be applied powerfully at home, in communities and in organisations everywhere.

We desperately need leaders who can lead. We need *amplifiers*— those leaders who can reduce fear and replace it with confidence, and reduce confusion and replace it with clarity, mobilising us all in pursuit of a better future. Motivational leadership is not a 'nice to do': it's a necessity, and one that becomes increasingly needed as we move further into a technological age where we find ourselves time poor and information rich. We need leaders who can take this data deluge and provide meaning, engagement and relevance around all the stuff that matters.

We need amplifiers.

That need is critical now as the world faces an unprecedented rate of change. In his essay *The Future of Work*, Jeff Brenman, futurist and designer from Apollo Ideas, says: 'we are teaching our kids to prepare for jobs that have not been invented yet, solving problems we don't even know we have yet'.

This era of massive disruption requires less long-term know-how and more immediate do now! Now more than at any other time in history we need to be able to adapt quickly; we need to shift what we are doing at a moment's notice, take in new information and make well-informed, rapid decisions.

In their book *Decisive: How to Make Better Choices in Life and Work*, brothers Dan and Chip Heath, change management consultants, share a framework for making decisions in this new world order. They believe we need a process that saves us from ourselves when it comes to making great decisions. They describe a range of 'villains' that prevent us from making good decisions:

> If you think about a normal decision process, it usually proceeds in four steps:
>
> - You encounter a choice. But narrow framing makes you miss options.
>
> - You analyze your options. But the confirmation bias leads you to gather self-serving information.
>
> - You make a choice. But short-term emotion will often tempt you to make the wrong one.
>
> - Then you live with it. But you'll often be overconfident about how the future will unfold.
>
> And what we've seen is that there is a villain that afflicts each of these stages.

Amplifiers are discerning, they spend time helping people make better decisions. Creel Price, author of *The One Thing to Win at the Game of Business*, calls leadership 'decisionship' because, in his entrepreneurial experience, making decisions is the essence of leadership.

Amplifiers support decision making as a business and leadership imperative. Decisions lead to actions, actions lead to results, results lead to beliefs, which then go on to affect choices. It's critical to make motivational leadership be about what gets done — otherwise it really is just talk.

We need change makers not change managers. Amplifiers are absolute change makers. They agitate and stir the ponds of complacency and communicate vision in a dynamic, engaging and relevant way so that all are on board, in the right seats and heading on the same journey.

Strategy, it seems, is failing many, as it is almost impossible to create solutions for futures further out than 12 to 36 months. History may end up recording this current era as the Age of Disruption: computer companies are killing music companies; disintermediation (the removal of the middle man) is destroying brokerage businesses; and geo-arbitrage (low-cost labour) is killing age-old 'safe' careers such as accounting and law. We are most definitely living in interesting times.

Make no mistake — strategy is critical. It's simply not all that it's been made out to be. It is an analytical idea and as such lives in the left hemisphere of the brain, whereas culture is less specific and lives in the right hemisphere. The famous statement by US general George Patton sums it up: 'A good plan, violently executed now, is better than a perfect plan next week'. Strategy is a great start; it is simply a good plan, though, if the culture that implements it lacks the ability to execute.

Cynthia Montgomery, in her book *The Strategist: Be the Leader Your Business Needs*, makes the case for the synergistic relationship between leaders and strategy. Montgomery's concern is that strategy has been outsourced to experts and advisers, to the detriment of business. She suggests that the fixed nature of strategy that most organisations adopt is flawed: 'What's been forgotten is that strategy is not a destination or a solution. It's not a problem to be solved and settled. It's a journey. It needs continuous, not intermittent, leadership'.

Motivational leadership—amplification—trumps strategy every time. Boston Consulting Group, in their *Creating People Advantage* report, reference the power of culture and people management as the 'single biggest issue facing business leaders today'. This theme is picked up again and again in leadership texts. Corporate anthropologist and author of *Finding True North*, Michael Henderson, a global culture expert, states that in his research he has found 'culture to be eight times more powerful than strategy'.

In other words, the wrong people doing the right stuff is significantly less important than the right people doing the wrong stuff. In a logic-filled, post-industrial world it's easy to see why the head of business (strategy) has been given a lead role. It's time for the heart of business and society (culture) to take its place.

Amplification—motivational leadership—is the link between the two. It acts like the corpus callosum in the brain—a thick band of axons (nerve fibres) that connects the right hemisphere to the left hemisphere. It is the missing link between strategy—what we know we should do and attitude (the willingness to do it)—and execution (getting it done).

Motivational leadership is the quality we need to see in the conversations taking place everywhere, from the office corridors to the classrooms in schools, from the boardroom to the ballrooms in business, and from the bedrooms to the kitchen table in homes.

Someone has to lead.

This book will make the case for raising your levels of motivational leadership at home, in your community and in your business. It's a call to arms for developing the intent to influence; it's an invitation to become an amplifier.

Famous motivational speaker the late Zig Ziglar highlighted the impermanence of motivation during an interview with an adversarial journalist. The journalist, keen to establish the moniker of hype-merchant on Mr Ziglar asked, 'Mr Ziglar, this motivation thing you peddle — it's not permanent is it?'

To which Zig replied, in his Texan drawl:

> No son, motivation is not permanent, but then again neither is sanitation! And based on the proximity of our corporal selves in this interview and the absence of a noticeable stench, you must have washed today? And that being the case it is highly likely you will do so again, tomorrow and the next day? Occasionally you miss a day but you are quick to resume the habit. Motivation is most definitely not permanent and that's why it's critical you get into the habit of using it daily.

This book contends that, if you are responsible for others, you may as well leave the shower running continuously. If not, you will develop an attitudinal odour, a stinking thinking, and the people you lead will require a 'check up from the neck up' to cure the organisational infection that steals hope, belief and fortitude. (Channelled a bit of Zig in that last line, I reckon.)

The book's premise is quite simple: learn how to use motivational leadership to get things done in and around you. Get really good at being an amplifier: it's not just talk and you do make a difference!

The problem is that while the principles of motivational leadership are simple, the application of them requires some art, some finesse and no small amount of courage. It takes courage to stand up and shine a light. It is way too easy to leave that to others. There will always be cowards in the dark who take pot shots at those who shine a light on the path of others. One thing though is universally true — you cannot hold a torch to light another's path without also illuminating your own.

This book is divided into four parts. Part I describes the history and case for motivational leadership. It is an exposé or thought piece on the role of motivational leadership throughout history, and the power of motivational leadership to effect change and make the world a better place. Think of this as the *why* and *if* of being an amplifier.

Part II expounds the art and science for developing motivational leadership. Think of part II as the *how* and part III as the *what* and part IV as the *who* of being an amplifier.

If you are already a convert to motivational leadership, you can jump straight into part II and get to work increasing your amplification skills. If you remain unconvinced but open and willing, then let's get started working through the *why* in greater detail.

Part I

THE WHY

Every story begins with why. Why this topic, why now, why am I writing it, why would you read it? There are a lot of whys that need our attention. The big idea here, in part I, is that there is a leadership progression, a leadership ladder if you like, that charts the ideal leader's journey. A journey that begins with technical competence and personal greatness, and very quickly flips 180 degrees and becomes about developing those same qualities of greatness in others.

Your career starts with technical competence; you get good at something; often you then end up managing others; and if you are on track you can then end up in positions of leadership taking responsibility for the decisions and direction of your enterprise, be it social, personal or organisational.

It's at this point you have three evolving choices. The first is the choice to motivate others or not; to engage with people, help them be the best they can and do the best work they can — the choice of motivational leadership. The second choice is a tough one as it requires a certain acceptance that who you are and how you go about your day may act as inspiration for others; this is the choice to be inspirational. It's the third choice that has the single most important impact on a group. This is the choice to amplify, to take the motivated and help them become motivators, to not only be inspiring but inspire others to do the same. To teach the teachers and create the leaders who then in turn will do the same. You become an amplifier!

CHAPTER I

Do we need leaders?

Your answer to the question of whether we need leaders is probably the critical juncture in this book, so I may as well start by asking it outright: do we need leaders?

For me the answer is, 'Yes, absolutely, without a shadow of a doubt'.

This may not be the case for everyone. I was once asked in an interview whether there really was a need for one person to motivate another and that surely it is the realm of each person to find their own motivation for why they do what they do. Seems logical, but this statement is flawed. Motivation is definitely intrinsic, but inspiration is not. Your job as a motivational leader is not to *do* something that motivates others but rather to *be* something to others. Maybe you are a sounding board; maybe you are a navigator; or maybe you are a shining light. These three metaphors set out the role of the leader in an inspired culture, one that is rich in motivational leadership.

The leadership ladder

In this book we are climbing a ladder where leadership grows up (see figure 1.1, overleaf). The impact of leadership and its influence is felt in increasing doses. Each stage on the leadership ladder is iterative and inclusive. We take the best of the previous stage with us to the next, and we can't get to the higher levels without these firmly in place. It's hard to measure good leadership because, by their very nature, great leaders should pass the scoreboard and credit onto others. While leadership is hard to define, its absence is keenly felt.

Figure 1.1: the leadership ladder

Label	Influence	Focus	Attitude	Impact	Action
Amplifiers	Transformational	Results	Build the capability to do even more	1:22 500	Deploy
Inspirers	Inspirational	Will	Give us the will to do more	1:1500	Leverage
Motivators	Motivational	Big why	Help us know why we are doing it	1:150	Maximise
Leaders	Directional	Where	Share where we are heading	1:50	Develop
Managers	Managerial	How	Know how best to do it	1:25	Engage
Technicians	Functional	What	Know what's next	1:5	Nurture
Demotivators	Dysfunctional	Little why	Create a culture of 'why bother?'	1:0	Change
Vacuum	Absent	Who	Create a culture of 'who cares?'	0:0	Address

Great leaders motivate, exceptional leaders inspire, transformational leaders amplify. They amplify the best of what's in themselves and around them. How good at amplification are you?

Amplifiers are the rare leaders who bring out leadership in others. They are the masters of maximising potential and turning it into talent. Amplifiers are able to attract, retain and develop other great leaders. They spend their life bringing out the best in others. This book explores why they matter and how you can develop your levels of amplification.

Like ripples in a pond the effect of an amplifier in an organisation can be hard to quantify but their impact is quantum. Their absence keenly felt. Amplifiers are the leaders worth following, who help us do work worth doing and create cultures worth belonging to.

The vacuum

A leadership vacuum is something that many people can instantly iden-tify. Without anyone in charge things start to get really random, really fast. A leadership vacuum creates a massive disengagement, as people randomly focus on whatever they want that serves their self-interest.

It's not unlike the situation in the famous William Golding novel *Lord of the Flies*. This is a story about a group of British boys stuck on an uninhabited island who try to govern themselves, with disastrous results. It explores the already controversial subjects of human nature and individual welfare versus the common good.

It's hard for these kids, without some amplifiers, to care about anything beyond their current selfish world view. But this is what amplifiers do — they help us to see possibilities that we can't see ourselves. They are custodians of better possible futures. They hold a belief in what we can do individually and collectively, and are able to help align personal interests with the common good. All in a gentle, custodial way, as opposed to a superior and controlled way.

You may argue that the boys in Golding's novel have leaders — the alpha kids who form cabals, and hunt down and murder the weaker children. That's the distinction between leadership alone and amplification. Amplifiers are able to elevate the game; in a way they are shifting the collective consciousness in a particular direction. They have a positive intent to influence.

In her great book *Followership*, leadership contrarian Barbara Kellerman makes the obvious statement that each leader needs at least one follower. She goes on to say that the traditional view of leadership should be put to the sword. She argues that with all the massively disruptive social change of the past 10 to 50 years, leadership as we knew it is dead or dying. She claims that we need to become less leader-centric and more follower-centric.

Amplifiers make the world better for people personally and, at the same time, advance collective group goals. Traditional leaders drive strategy, but often the people get left behind. Amplifiers know that leadership is personal and that, not only do people matter, but focused in the right way they are also the difference between success and failure.

The bad

If you have ever worked for a jerk you know the detrimental impact a bad leader can have on a group. Nothing saps the energy of good people more quickly than bad leaders. They are the adults who have never grown up. These people somehow work their way through the rank and file, and end up in positions of influence. They bully; they blame; and they basically allow their personal pathology to drive their leadership behaviours.

Like many dysfunctional personalities they often create unhelpful co-dependent relationships. You will often see a demotivator in some kind of odd power partnership with others whose own personal weakness causes them to align with an idiot in charge. It's human nature, but it's not our best nature. A bully's buddy is often as damaging as the bully, for the simple act of affirmation that they give the bad leader. It causes you at worst to question whether you may have it wrong—maybe nice guys don't get the corner office?—or at best to simply give up on trying to do anything about it. Both the bully leader and their buddy are below the line: they are not even really on the ladder.

These unleaders demotivate and create toxic cultures. We may be better off taking our chances with no leader than one of these. We should actively eliminate these people from our teams: ruthlessly educate them to free up their future and go play somewhere else. They are the attitudinal equivalent of toxic waste. They kill anything good that's going on within a group.

If you are on the leadership ladder and reading this book, then you are willing to do work on yourself. Amplifiers know that the speed of change within a group is directly proportional to firstly the leader's own personal growth and then the growth of the individuals within the group. They have the courage to stay open, to keep learning and to keep reshaping who they become as they do.

Carol Dweck in her book *Mindset* unpacks the case for what she names 'fixed' versus 'growth' mindsets. She makes a brilliant case for the danger of becoming too rigid in your thinking, too reliant on your strengths and talents. She argues that success is more about being able to work hard and develop capability than about having or not having a talent and acting accordingly:

> In short, when people believe in fixed traits, they are always in danger of being measured by a failure. It can define them in a permanent way. Smart or talented as they may be, this mindset seems to rob them of their coping resources. When people believe their basic qualities can be developed, failures may still hurt, but failures don't define them.

Amplifiers have a growth mindset and the belief that with hard work and focus many things we think are impossible are actually very possible. Not in a woo-hoo, magical, 'you can be anything you want' way, but rather just the expectation that work creates results. Amplifiers not only help people believe more in themselves, but also create the environment in which they can become the best possible version of themselves.

The smart

We need to get the technically competent people in any group to be involved. Those with the specific subject matter expertise to know what to do and how to go about getting it done are critical to the success of the group. Without those who know how-to we end up being a group full of promise but with little ability to deliver on goals and objectives. Without the technicians, all a group can do is just talk.

Back in the days of artisans and master craftsmen, specialised practical knowledge was the prized commodity in the community. Industrialisation marginalised these roles, and now as we emerge into developed economies with knowledge-based and service-based industries, a new type of technician has emerged. In software engineering they are called 'whitesmiths' for their ability to create, in code, great tools and solutions for getting things done. They are the modern-day blacksmiths. We need the technicians to participate in the group goals.

Amplifiers don't try to be the smartest person in the room: rather they help others to step into that role. It was Henry Ford (industrialist and entrepreneur) who said, 'surround yourself with people smarter than you and get out of the way'. Enrol, harness and develop the smart technicians; don't compete with them.

The focused

Management gets a bad name in many business books. It's represented as a kind of cardigan-wearing, boring compliance function. It is, however, the essential next rung in the motivational leadership journey. The management function was made common by the lean process engineering of the industrial revolution. In management talk, humans become assets—resources that we manage for maximum efficiency.

Levels of management drive accountability and compliance, which in turn drives efficiency. We need managers to get things done, but as management alone often ends up being a resource leverage war you will find yourself with stress and be overwhelmed if all you have is management to rely upon. Managers are brilliant at activating the people around them to get the job done; they marshal resources and get people focused.

The drivers

Leaders are the ones who provide direction. They answer the question Where are we heading? We need to develop leaders at all levels in our groups. Leadership is not always positional, as in a job description or a line on a business card. Peter Baines, author of *Hand Across the Water* and a leadership expert, calls it 'leadership without authority'—that person who steps into the breach when required. Speaking about leadership in crisis and leading several tours of disaster victim identification crews, Baines knows first hand about leadership under fire.

It's my belief that most progressive groups have a mix of technicians, managers and leaders. These first three productive rungs on the leadership ladder are Business 101. Activate your technicians; harness your scarce resources through managers; and engage people with the vision with great leaders. Do this and you will get an active culture: one that is strategic in its approach and aligned in its efforts—all 'good stuff'.

It's in this development of people from technician, through to manager and on to leader that many organisations traditionally invest huge amounts of time, money and energy into. Often called a leadership pipeline, it's a smart process but it's missing one final shift. It's an essential effort and piece of work, but it does stink of effort. There are, however, gravities at work that prevent organisations from moving people up the ladder as quickly or as widely as you, the leader, may wish. That's the shift opportunity that amplifiers create. If we move from the simple formal process of moving our technicians to managers to one where we develop their leadership, and help them understand the power of motivational leadership, then we get massive shifts and significant results.

Motivators: the tipping point

Motivational leaders are able to engage the people around them to achieve the objectives of the group. A 'leaderful' organisation is one in which people know what to do, are actively doing it and are progressing towards identified goals.

Essentially, motivational leadership is a tipping point. By developing magnetic leaders who are able to maximise the efforts of a small group of people—creating joy and magic moments within a business—you get a leadership lift.

In sailing, you can turn the yacht into a gust of wind and get either a lift or a lull. A lull is when the wind fights your forward progress; a lift is when you get to 'work up' closer to the mark. A lift in racing becomes a competitive advantage. You don't rely on it, but you most definitely look for it and use it whenever you can. Leadership lifts are not permanent, but they are significant. Achieving leadership lifts is the unspecified but critical job role of the motivational leader and the first step of three. Plenty of books, strategies and courses exist for the lower stages of the leadership ladder, but it's the last three that start to have significant new impacts on business and that's the focus of this book.

The inspirers

New generations of self-directed, if not self-actualised, individuals need less external motivation to get things done and rather are in pursuit of inspiration. They are looking to learn from, emulate and maybe even slingshot past inspiring leaders who help them get more of what they want. The etymology of the word inspiration is to 'breathe life into'. This is what inspiring leaders do. They are, quite literally, breaths of fresh air. The impact of an inspiring leader on a group is massive. When such a group leaves a room, they are more confident, more clear in their minds and most definitely charged to do something.

The amplifiers

Amplifiers are a new level in the leadership ladder, distinguishable from other levels by their ability to develop motivators and inspirers, and not just be one themselves. In tech terms they are the new operating system. They take all the best bits of the previous five positive stages on the leadership ladder and add a final quality: multiplication. They are not only motivating, they also create motivators; they are not only inspiring, they inspire inspirers. They go from being the smartest and most inspiring in the room, to actually breeding those qualities in others. Their effect is exponential. If one motivator can reach 150 people, and an amplifier creates 150 motivators, the amplifier can indirectly reach 22 500 people. They have exponential and immeasurable impacts on communities and businesses.

Amplification represents the final step of the three new levels of leadership, starting with motivational leadership, and followed by inspirational leadership and amplified leadership. They bring the work, the leadership and the culture together. This affects strategy and productivity, and execution and engagement, and drives innovation and sustainable high performance.

Key assumptions

Before we launch into the amplifier story any further I want to share some key assumptions or beliefs that are driving this conversation. A cleverly worded argument can convince you against your will (at least for a while) that something is true, when it may actually not be true for you. The key to understanding any school of thought is to understand the underlying assumptions behind it. This allows us to agree in principle first before we agree in practice. This book is heavily oriented to actual practices you can undertake to build a more leaderful organisation. But before we go into all that, let's test my assumptions against your beliefs.

It's my hope that by making these assumptions explicit I will be able to increase the number of smart sceptics who become evangelists for the amplifier movement.

Here are the underlying assumptions to the amplifier movement:

- Leaders make a difference.
- We develop leadership in and around us.
- More leaders are better than fewer leaders.
- Leadership is a choice.
- People are good.

Leaders make a difference

This whole book is predicated on the idea that leaders matter, that we need them and that an individual can make a difference.

The anti-argument is that people will easily self-organise, that they don't need direction and that left to their own devices they will create significant results.

Testing your assumptions	Yes or No	
Do leaders matter?	☐	☐
Do leaders make a difference to the success of a group?	☐	☐
Are we better off with leaders?	☐	☐

We develop leadership in and around us

Many people believe that leaders are born not made. *Amplifiers* says that leadership can be developed and that it is a choice more than a capability.

The anti-argument is that leaders are born that way, that you cannot develop leadership traits, that leadership is preordained and you are fated to be a follower or a leader.

Testing your assumptions	Yes or No	
Can leadership be developed?	☐	☐
Can talents be developed—are they not fixed?	☐	☐
Could you be a better leader?	☐	☐

More leaders are better than fewer leaders

Amplifiers are not just motivational leaders, they are not simply inspiring role models—they are the DNA of future leaders. They focus on bringing out greatness in others and as a result amplify the results tenfold (or more). They fill leadership pipelines and are responsible for developing leadership succession inside an organisation.

The anti-argument is that 'too many cooks spoil the broth'. We are better off seeding control to a few good men and women, and deferring the responsibility up the hierarchical chain of command. Summed up as 'not my job' or 'that's why you get paid the big bucks!'

Testing your assumptions	**Yes or No**	
Is decentralising leadership a good thing?	☐	☐
Is giving more responsibility to people at all levels in an organisation smart?	☐	☐
Do you believe that transparency leads to ownership?	☐	☐

Leadership is a choice

Leadership is not positional. It's not about your given authority: it's about the decision to lift *your* game and *the* game. It's about making choices to operate with personal responsibility—to step up to the plate and say 'I've got it!'

The anti-argument is that we have leaders to make decisions and that we don't need the majority of people to understand why or how: they simply need to do what they are told to do. It's about people doing their work with very little say in the matter.

Testing your assumptions	**Yes or No**	
Can you be a leader even if you have no authority?	☐	☐
Is leadership a choice? Can anyone choose leadership?	☐	☐
Do you have control in life around what you do about what happens to you?	☐	☐

People are good

A cynical view of the world has you managing others from a 'people will rip you off' frame of reference. Amplification is about operating from the assumption that given a positive purpose (work worth doing) and an environment that you feel you belong to (culture worth belonging to) and someone you can respect (leaders worth following) almost anyone will respond and work from a good place rather than a bad one.

Make no mistake: there are always sociopaths and people with bad behavior traits, but essentially good trumps bad. The underlying assumption is that most people in the world are good people, doing no conscious harm to others and wanting what we all want: something to do, someone to love and something to hope for.

The anti-argument is that people can't be trusted. Left to their own devices they will steal staplers, spend time on Facebook and try to rip off the system.

Testing your assumptions	Yes or No	
Are people just like you in most cases?	☐	☐
Do you believe most people want to do good work and are not lazy?	☐	☐
Is building others up not only a good thing to do, but also an effective thing?	☐	☐

If you are okay with these assumptions then let's go, let's get it done; no more discussion really needs to be entered into. We simply have to take the necessary steps to draw people up the leadership ladder to be difference makers — amplifiers. Move straight to part II.

Mahatma Gandhi said, 'My life is an invisible whole, and all my activities run into one another; and they have their rise in my insatiable love of mankind.'

Sceptics versus cynics

I love sceptics. One of my favourites is *Skeptic* magazine founder Michael Shermer, whose book *Why People Believe Weird Things* is a humorous and telling exposé of the evolutionary and cognitive basis for crazy lapses in reason. Shermer also delivered a fabulous presentation on TED.com about the power of scepticism. You can watch the video on the *Amplifiers* website: www.amplifiersthebook.com.

My time at university was in the science faculty, so I have a healthy respect for the scientific approach and the idea that a sceptic suspends judgement until they have gathered all the facts. To be a sceptic is essentially a good thing. It's about resisting the latest trend or fashionable thought and instead looking at the underlying proposition that sits behind any communication. I know you are reading this book right now and you have not skipped straight to part II. Thanks for hanging in here. This is important.

In some texts on the topics of culture and motivation, it has been suggested that you need to remove nay-sayers from your team. The standard argument goes that negative people bring the team down. Sometimes a sceptic is labelled negative when they simply question the leader's decisions or thinking. This seems inherently dangerous. It simply makes sense that the higher the stakes and the more complex the issues in a business, community or culture, the more you need many heads working towards a common solution. No doubt the responsibility for a decision is the leader's, but some healthy dissent and robust discussion is not a bad thing.

Salerno and the notion of SHAM

On the topic of dissent, probably the biggest critic of anything at all that smells like personal development is Steve Salerno, an investigative journalist. In his book *SHAM, Self-Help and Actualization Movement: How the Gurus of the Self-Help Movement Make Us Helpless*, Salerno makes the case for the negative impact of what he calls the hype-based hope merchants of the self-help movement. He is of the opinion, and makes a compelling case, that much of what is said in the personal development and self-help movement is actually counterproductive and likely to hold a person back. He identifies the self-help actualisation movement as a SHAM.

As an investigative journalist, he cites reasons as to why it's destructive to the US psyche — which he defines as the prevailing mindset and approach to dealing with adversity — to proliferate the lessons of 'You can do it'. You have to hear him out, though, because he is spot on: the turkeys and over the top motivational leaders are destructive. They are just talk and they don't make a positive difference in the long run. They deserve our ridicule and should be dismissed out of hand.

Besides, it's easy to pick on their larger than life promises and often subsequent falls from grace as the relationship expert goes through their second marriage; the weight loss guru is caught nicking doughnuts; and the wealth creation guru turns out to have built their wealth on a Ponzi confidence scheme that collapses like a house of cards. In each example there is an actual guru we could name who has done exactly that. Is it any wonder that smart people resist the empty rah-rah behind the bad iterations of motivational leadership?

One of the targets for Salerno's investigation is the 12-step Alcoholics Anonymous program. Salerno has identified five underlying premises in the program that he thinks are flawed and which undermine any good that AA may do. His summary is useful, as it lets you know the dangerous shoals a motivational leader can pass through on their way to well-meaning good amplification. The five flawed premises behind AA's 12-step program that he has identified are:

Salerno's premise 1: You are broken.

Salerno's premise 2: Good is bad.

Salerno's premise 3: It's all about you.

Salerno's premise 4: All suffering is created equal.

Salerno's premise 5: It's not your fault.

My disclaimer 1: I reckon AA does great work

I want to be crystal clear: Alcoholics Anonymous, to my mind, does great work. Understanding, as I do from my formal education, the chemical triggers and dopamine gaps in the minds of addicts, I have huge respect for anyone who spends a lifetime resisting alcohol. And I am talking about legitimate addicts with significant chemical imbalances, and not Hollywood bad boys and girls who go in and out of rehab, treating it like a health spa.

I do love what we can learn from these messages and the mindset Salerno comes from—they are so helpful for the students of amplification. They don't have to be accurate to be useful.

My disclaimer 2: Salerno's opinions are not mine

What I want to do is use Salerno's key premises as platforms that bring motivational leadership up to date, and keep it relevant and authentic. His view is valid as it picks the holes in simple motivational rhetoric. It's important to move away from the simplistic rah-rah of the 1980s motivational speaker and see the issues as multifaceted. The amplifier needs the intelligent leaders to engage with their agenda and can't rely on simply 'you can do it' arguments to do so.

Salerno's premise 1: You are broken

Amplifier alternative: let's instead focus on 'you are talented'.

The old paradigm of 'you are broken and I can fix you' drives 360 degree feedback, performance review and a lot of the self-help courses out there. Instead, let's make sure that we focus on the strengths and talents people have that can be utilised for greatness.

Salerno's premise 2: Good is bad

Amplifier alternative: let's build a bridge and get over our past.

'The paradigm of your past needs exploring and you carry emotional baggage from past trauma' is at the heart of Salerno's criticism. This is an important idea for motivational leaders. Exploring a team member's past is at best the realm of qualified psychotherapists and at worst just a whole bunch of self-indulgent excuse-making for why we can't get stuff done. Let's treat what may have happened to you or anyone of your amplifiers as lessons, not excuses. Rather than dwelling on the past as if we were victims of abuse, we may do better to build a bridge and get over it.

Salerno's premise 3: It's all about you

Amplifier alternative: let's be attention-out and of service to others.

Salerno suggests that the self-development 'me' work of the 1980s and the central idea in the co-dependent conversation of the 12-step program is flawed. He goes on to explore the isolating selfishness this creates. The last thing we want in organisations—right?

The upgrade here is to focus on serving yourself by serving others. A taxi driver once shared a definition of seduction to me (which was a surreal experience in itself). He said that sex is about pulling what you can out of a relationship, while seduction was about putting all you can into it. Put another way: help enough people get what they want and you will eventually get all that you want.

Salerno's premise 4: All suffering is created equal

Amplifier alternative: let's stop the drama—your biography is not your destiny.

Salerno points out that when we make *my* suffering as bad as yours we become obsessed with personally validating our 'traumas' as equally significant. Sufferers then eventually become immune to the drama of others and end up jaded, as they dismiss other people's pain as 'their shit, not mine'.

Motivational speaker Anthony Robbins, himself a target in Salerno's book, has the answer for this one. One of his primary teaching mantras is that 'your past does not equal your future'. This is the perfect response. Its focus is forward and outwards. It is forward into tomorrow and out from you. Your past does not equal your future. Build a bridge and get over it.

Salerno's premise 5: It's not your fault

Amplifier alternative: make it your responsibility.

Salerno hits this one on the head, and I love how he does it. I'll quote him directly on this one:

> Once you start making allowances (for people's bad behaviour) based on people's weaknesses, where do you draw the line? And who gets to draw it? If a person has no power over his or her weakness, how does society credibly decide whose weakness is tolerable and whose isn't? Having gone that far how does society justify blaming people, much less punishing them for acts that are beyond their control?

Lorna Patten, a communication expert and the creator of OPEN UP relationship methodology, explains the solution as the New Paradigm. She explains and teaches that we have to operate from the mindset that 'We are 100% responsible for the whole of our reality!' You can watch Lorna's video on the *Amplifiers* website. Go to www. amplifiersthebook.com and click on 'videos'.

Making amplification work

For amplification to work—for motivational leadership to penetrate a cynical and hopeless culture—you need to know the land mines. Salerno's five premises are great objections to motivational leadership and are likely to raise their ugly little heads. Don't be caught out, or fall prey to the essential intelligent complaint that lies within each. Let's be smart motivators, inspiring clever people to transform culture and deliver on what truly matters.

But really, it all boils down to one thing: Do you believe that leadership matters? If you don't, then stop reading, get a refund and move on. If you do, then the cynics' arguments are irrelevant. It's the sceptics that we need to focus on.

The evidence is pretty strong and compelling: leaders do matter! History is filled with examples of men and women who stood up for something, who led a group and changed the course and direction of history. I once watched Simon Sinek, author of *Start with Why*, speak with elegant simplicity on leadership. He said that you need only one thing for leadership to exist—followers—and that the key to activating followers is to start with 'why'? Simon's formal training included anthropology, the study of effective culture and how it prevails.

Motivational leadership is the start (the big why); inspirational leadership is the next (it creates the will); and deploying amplifiers is the ultimate step on this journey, as it builds leadership legacy and future by focusing on results.

This training is summed up by another famous 'anthro', Margaret Mead, who famously said: 'Never underestimate the power of a small group of people to change the world; indeed it's the only thing that ever has'.

Motivational leadership directs this energy for change. If a leader needs followers, then groups need more than simply direction. They need to be mobilised towards better futures. Linking all of this are powerful amplifiers.

Amplifiers are not only okay with the sceptics—they target them. Get a sceptic on board and huge amounts of power come from their intellectual endorsement.

So let's be clear—sceptics are good!

Cynics are bad

It's the cynics we must develop a zero tolerance for. A cynic is someone who has given up, but has not yet shut up. These are those people who are actively disengaged and working against the positive movement of the group. Often a cynic was an idealist who has allowed their hopes to be crushed, and they are now bitter and twisted against the world.

How can we recognise the difference?

The sceptic:

- tells you to your face that an idea is flawed and works with you on the solution
- gathers all the facts before deciding
- is happy for you to ignore their opinion as long as you consider it.

The cynic:

- talks an idea down in your absence
- has made up their mind before any facts are gathered or shared
- needs their opinion to be the decision you make.

Amplifiers are—and the act of amplification is—an act of love. If you struggle with the word 'love' it will be hard to be a great amplifier. Fall in love with love. Take the idea of love and let it instruct all that you do. Any time you take an act against another ask yourself is this an act of love, or is it something else.

I will leave off the development of love for others to write and teach about. Tough love, loving what we do, loving each other, loving ourselves and loving our customers, loving our products, loving our team—all good comes from love.

Okay, I ain't the love doctor, so let's move on.

Positive versus optimistic

Amplification is not about developing an attitude of blind positivity. It's most definitely about the power of hope and brighter futures, but it does not ignore the harsh realities that may exist in which people are right. A bus may hit a blindly positive person and they rosily say 'Oh well, I needed some time off'. That's not what this is about. This is more about optimism, a trait that can be learned and developed.

Leading psychologist and behavioural science researcher Martin Seligman, has made a career out of researching the idea that optimism can be learned. Here he explains the two key ideas behind being optimistic:

> Whether or not we have hope depends on two dimensions of our explanatory style; pervasiveness and permanence. Finding temporary and specific causes for misfortune is the art of hope: Temporary causes limit helplessness in time, and specific causes limit helplessness to the original situation...The optimistic style of explaining good events is the opposite of that used for bad events: It's internal rather than external. People who believe they cause good things tend to like themselves better than people who believe good things come from other people or circumstances.

Optimism is about developing the habit of focusing on the productive thread of action. Asking the question, 'What can we do to move forward regardless of how dire things may be?' This is the critical focus point of amplifiers. The moment you turn a blind eye to the negatives and harsh realities of a tough situation you begin to lose traction. So, one eye on the bad and one eye on the good, and move towards the light. Sorry—that sounded way more biblical than intended.

The shift towards authenticity

A business or a leader can spend years building a reputation only to have it pulled down in a moment by a careless tweet or social media posting. A viral YouTube video shared by many can tell a truth that no amount of spin can cover up.

Peter Gabriel's WITNESS program puts videos in the hands of activists so they can report on human atrocity and crimes against humanity. Their mantra is 'See it. Film it. Change it'. The WITNESS mission explains what they do succinctly: 'Our Mission at WITNESS is to use video to open the eyes of the world to human rights violations. WITNESS empowers people to transform personal stories of abuse into powerful tools for justice, promoting public engagement and policy change'.

If you are faking it we will know: the truth will out.

Authenticity is not an option any more: morally it never should have been. We are in an era of greater transparency, and so there is a real mandate that we lead authentically. Customers can see further into businesses than ever before and mistakes live forever on Facebook.

Rather than worrying about the loss of secrecy or privacy, leaders could consider the importance of humility and vulnerability. It's time to tell the truth about what you are good at and what you are not so good at. The business leader, the social leader or family leader doesn't need to be perfect.

It's this quality of imperfection that creates interdependence and reliance (both good things) on others. A generation or two ago it was expected that a leader had all the answers in the room. You got to be the boss by being the smartest person in the room. Now it's clear that the leader is the one who brings out the brilliance in others—the amplifier.

It hasn't always been like this. In recent history we have seen a shift away from poster-perfect leaders to a more authentic human model. This shift is one in which leaders need to keep it real, own their mistakes, show their human side and be authentic leaders. Media scrutiny, freedom of the press and the ease with which any spectator can be a commentator has only accelerated this shift. In seconds a tweet, post or mobile phone video broadcast will unravel any carefully manicured projection of *you* as the perfect leader.

This shift towards authenticity is quite recent. If you contrast the era of John F. Kennedy with the era of Bill Clinton, you can see this shift played out quite publicly. They both had sexual relationships with 'a woman' other than their wife in the White House. In JFK's day no one talked about it and it was easier to keep a lid on it. Fast forward to Bill Clinton's fall from grace with intern Monica Lewinsky and you see a completely new world of transparency and accountability. It's not about being perfect any more, but it is about keeping it real and telling the truth.

This shift is most keenly felt in generational demographics. Generation Y—people born from 1980 through to about 1995—grew up through this period of greater public accountability and scrutiny. They created Facebook and work for Google, and are absolutely driven to a movement of openness. It's not really an argument about whether Facebook is good or bad, or whether privacy is lost. Unless you can get off the grid somehow and lose all your digital fingerprints you will be scrutinised! For Gen Y this is their normal.

Motivational leaders may be commented on more than the traditional leaders. If you start making noise, people who disagree with you will come out of the woodwork and start to throw rotten fruit at you. The minute you take a stand on something, those who disagree will appear.

That's kind of the point, isn't it? Just don't let that stop you.

Civil rights leader Martin Luther King Jr famously said:

> Cowardice asks the question, Is it safe? Expediency asks the question, Is it politic? Vanity asks the question, Is it popular? But conscience asks the question, Is it right? And there comes a time when one must take a position that is neither safe, nor politic, nor popular, but he must take it because his conscience tells him it is right.

Courage is an essential quality in a leader. Courage says that you are taking action towards something you believe in, regardless of the consequences.

Speak your truth—stand for something!

The trick is not to find the perfect all-encompassing message that appeases all. It's rather about communicating what you believe with conviction, humility and an intention to serve. This way you can look a detractor in the eye and know your difference of opinion for what it is. This is why democratic communities encourage healthy debate and discourse. It is critical to intelligent influential leadership.

Leadership communication expert Jacquie Molloy is founder of the Debate Camp initiative, a leadership training program for board members that teaches them to use debate as a means of carrying out their board meetings. Molloy calls it like this:

> We have come to think of 'arguing' as a bad thing. We think of it as something to avoid because of the inherent discomfort (or discourtesy) we have attached to it. But an argument is also a type of rhetoric. It doesn't have to be an inflamed high-volume situation.
>
> In fact, the power of Debate is that it is an argument; an argument that is held within the frame of agreed rules of engagement. And it's because of this that it is a very effective way of exploring issues, handling differences of opinion and resolving disagreement.
>
> Debate is an exploration of (at least) two sides of an issue. It is a rich discussion that allows everyone 'at the table' the right to participate and allows for every position to be heard less space—in fact, it demands it. In a world that becomes more complex by the nano second, this can only be a good thing.
>
> Think of the boardroom. The most important function of the Board in its governance role is to make sound decisions in an environment that is rife with complexity and risk. The best possible precursor to sound decision-making is the discussion that allows the board to know when they have what they need to make a decision. The shallower the discussion—the riskier the decision. That's not a set-in-stone formula of course but it's a pretty good rule of thumb.
>
> If Debate is such a great way to explore issues, resolve disagreement and make better decisions, why aren't we better at it?
>
> There are a few reasons and not all of them are logical. In the main, we tend to consider Debate as old-fashioned and a bit starchy. Or when we do think of them in current practice we call two models to mind: parliamentary debates (which often seem like a forum for bad behaviour and insults) and presidential debates (which often appear as though neither candidate is listening to the other; they're just waiting to deliver the next section of their 'stump speech').

But the main reason we don't draw on the power of Debate is that we lack the basic skills and knowledge. We lack the confidence to know how.

Boards and Exec Teams have so much to gain from adopting the practice of Debate. Effective decision making in the boardroom requires the articulation of ideas and points and views, and the careful listening to, and acceptance of, different ideas. Unfortunately for the majority of Boards, poor group dynamics, or a Chair who doesn't know how to get a far-reaching discussion 'back in the box' and when to transition into decision-making mode, prevent them from making this shift on their own.

So stand up, speak out and focus on positive action. Call out the cowardice and encourage the strength in others. Seriously, once the mechanical management compliance part of your job is done, what else is there?

CHAPTER 2

Grey matter

In my final argument for amplifiers, I am going to pull in some heavy hitters and drop some brain science on you. If neuroanatomy turns you on then read on. If not—then you have to take my word for it: your brain works better when you are inspired to believe and this makes everything you want to see happen in and around you more likely.

Let's look at the brain itself first. The human brain is complex, massively connected and dynamic, but for our purposes a simplified model of the brain is enough (see figure 2.1, overleaf). The brain consists of three major components: the brain stem and cerebellum (known as the reptilian brain), the limbic system (mammalian brain) and the cortex and neocortex (human brain). These are not brains in their own right but, from an evolutionary standpoint, they evolved (and grow in the womb) in this order, and the first two are derived from even earlier evolutionary forms.

The reptilian brain has been in evolutionary development for hundreds of millions of years and is very, very efficient at what it does. It controls automatic processes, such as body temperature and heart rate, and this is where we store habits (actually in the cerebellum, the cabbage-shaped protuberance in figure 2.1, overleaf). Anything that we do repetitively will be turned into a habit so that it can be repeated without conscious thought. Much of what we do is made up of habits: getting out of bed, showering, dressing, having breakfast, driving to work. Fight or flight responses are managed from here, along with the control of rage—the sudden, impulsive response to an external stimulus.

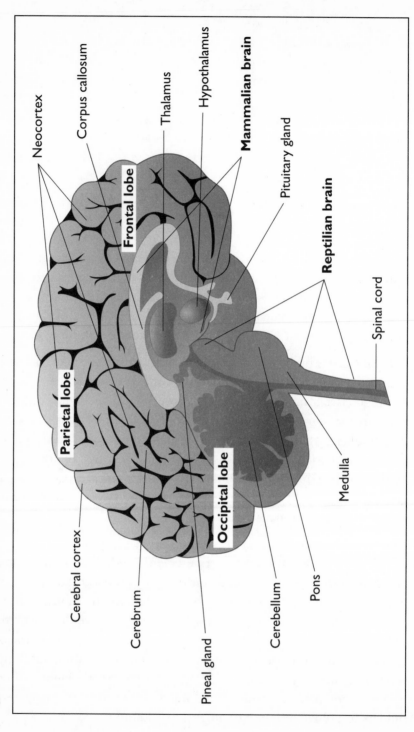

Figure 2.1: the structure of the human brain

The mammalian brain evolved more than 60 million years ago to allow adult mammals to have feelings for their offspring, and vice versa. So this is the source of emotions, feelings and moods plus emotional memory. Long-term memory is also located here, as is our ability to learn from experience. The mammalian brain is pre-verbal so we 'feel' this effect, sometimes called intuition. When we become expert at something and simply 'know' what to do, then it is the mammalian part of the brain at work. It is surprisingly powerful, given its relative size, and many of our decisions are made here.

The human brain has, at most, a few hundred thousand years of evolution behind it. It is enormously powerful, but rather energy intensive and inefficient. This is the seat of awareness—including our ability to deepen our awareness—and our self-identity. We manage our impulses from here. This is where we can imagine a future different from today, plan to get there and monitor how well our plans are unfolding. This is where we can share our plans with others through language, and incorporate feedback. We can think and solve problems, and we can act as social beings. This part of the brain is not fully developed physically until adulthood.

Brain structure and behaviour

Not long ago I was fortunate to sit with John Corrigan and the team from the Blue Brain Movement, a group dedicated to changing how education is led. They are a group on a mission to remove fear from schools and make learning not only safe but also more effective.

John and his colleagues from the Blue Brain Movement have unpacked some fascinating facts about the brain in action. Drawing on neuroscience they contend that the removal of fear is one of the single most important jobs of a leader. Their work has centred mainly on leadership in a learning environment, but it transfers directly into every environment where leadership matters—government, social, personal, educational and yes, organisational.

John and the team from the Blue Brain Movement have taken a complex idea and made it very accessible. I asked John to share his thoughts in this chapter as the ideas here are central, I think, to being an amplifier.

He talks about people being in the red zone and the blue zone of the brain. The red zone is the mind state that is based on our reptilian and mammalian brains and which dominates, even in adulthood, whenever we feel anxious, attacked, emotionally vulnerable and scared.

While we have the full range of emotional responses available to us, the ones people tend to focus on are based on responding to threat (real or imagined), fear or loss. And if unchecked, in the absence of the higher level awareness and control provided by the neocortex, we could massively increase further negative thoughts, feelings, moods, behaviour and even self-perception.

All in all, being in the red zone is not a useful state for higher level thinking and functioning.

In the blue zone we are optimistic, collaborative and creative. Our emotions are largely positive and we can handle complex tasks, including higher order learning. In the red zone we tend towards anxiety, pessimism and self-centredness. We tend to generalise about our condition and we can only handle simple tasks effectively. The blue zone uses the whole brain (the reptilian, mammalian and human brains), where everything is in its proper place and the locus of control resides with the neocortex or thinking brain.

As with the red zone, the full range of emotional responses are available. But the critical capacity of the neocortex allows us to think logically about choices as well as to think about our emotions themselves at a meta level.

It is in the blue zone where true learning takes place, and this is the state we should strive to live in.

And, most importantly, you cannot be in both zones simultaneously! You are either in control of your emotions and actions (blue zone) or you're not (red zone).

The red zone/blue zone idea provides a simple but effective metaphor that helps make sense of the power of engagement. If you want to influence anyone (child, adult, politician or friend) in any kind of positive way—they need to be in their blue brain. This is essentially the pre-knowledge for amplification — the thing that needs to be in effect to make amplification work.

It is helpful to superimpose the red zone/blue zone concept on top of the model of the brain. The blue zone involves resources being held in the human and mammalian brains, and the red zone involves resources being held in the mammalian and reptilian brains. In both states we have access to feelings and emotions, but these feelings and emotions are coloured by the accompanying brain element.

Most people have experienced both mind states. The easiest way to get into the blue zone is to get a good book and sit in front of a roaring fire (or a setting sun!) with a drink in hand. We have all experienced the red zone mind state. Standing in a supermarket queue and seeing all the other queues move more quickly will usually do it. We tend to think such things as 'this always happens to me' — a typical red zone, pessimistic and self-centred response.

One final but important point: our brains are designed to detect difference, and this ability is linked directly to the reptilian brain. We have probably all had the experience of walking into a room and thinking something has changed, something is different, and then looking around to find out what (for example, a picture has been removed). This ability switches resources into the primitive part of the brain and means that a red zone that is kept active can be 'switched on' by external triggers. From an evolutionary point of view this makes sense: if what we thought was a shadow turns out to be a predator, then we want to switch on fight or flight very quickly.

Nineteenth century education had the effect of holding a child's brain resources preferentially in the red zone and overdeveloping the habit-forming part of the brain (rote learning). As the brain is plastic, continual usage ensures using the brain in this way becomes the 'natural' way of using it. The adult becomes a habitual, obedient person. Having the red zone active means that 'difference' will trigger massive red zone activity and make such a person very resistant to change or even the contemplation of change, that is, anything different from what they know.

Education today generally has the effect of moving the child's resources between both the red and blue zones. When the child is conforming to what is required of them, the conditions are created for the child to operate in the blue zone and higher order learning can take place. The child engages with interesting and challenging content, which stimulates learning from experience. When the child is not conforming, the conditions for learning are withdrawn and the child's red zone is triggered. Our current systems can lead to high levels of learning while maintaining the red zone active—which means that people tend to be risk averse and uncreative and often have poor emotional intelligence. Children who come into school operating in their red zones (initiated from a home environment, for example) can often be kept there by their teachers and so little learning takes place for them. We see a persistent performance gap.

The forms of education that are struggling to emerge aim to hold the child's resources in the blue zone thus maximising the higher order learning that can take place. We get better academic outcomes when the child is operating in the blue zone. There is also a second effect, which is equally, if not more, important, and that is that a child held in a blue zone mind state can contemplate difficult, scary or challenging things (such as difference) without the red zone being triggered. If entering the blue zone is experienced a number of times, this ability will become a habit. In other words, the child will be able to contemplate difficult, scary or challenging things in the absence of the teacher and without the red zone being triggered. A child who is held in the blue zone will develop resilience (or 'character' as it used to be called)—the ability to face the vagaries of the world while staying in the optimal mind state to handle complex issues and change.

Both the 19th century and current education systems create dependent adults prone to anxiety—anxiety that can be allayed by strict certainty in the first case and via external support (for example, jobs-for-life, social security) under the original design for our current systems. The forms that are emerging create adults who are able to think and act independently and are able to live free of anxiety even under difficult and dangerous circumstances.

The key to holding a child in the blue zone is to have teachers operating fully in the blue zone. A small number do this already (the outstanding teachers that we can remember from our own schooling), but most do not, as they have been brought up under existing systems and continue to operate in the same way, even though the current system fails to meet the needs of our children and society's need for optimistic, collaborative, creative and resilient adults.

The key to making the shift is in creating a blue zone culture within a school, a culture within which adults operate in the blue zone as a matter of course. Just as children respond to the presence of a teacher operating in the blue zone by moving into the blue zone themselves, adults will too (which is how cognitive coaching works), so leaders operating in the blue zone are the means of creating such a culture.

Developing leaders—and ultimately teachers—to operate in this way is the means to make this transition, with leaders being the starting point.

Just as most people can be coached and can be trained to coach others, most leaders can be trained to behave in ways that draw other people into the blue zone. The effort required to behave in this way reduces the impact of the leader's own red zone, that is, they begin to operate more in the blue zone themselves. Thus it is possible to systematically create blue zone cultures within our schools and other organisations.

If you are keen to understand more about neuroanatomy and its effect on leadership, you may want to follow my good friend and leadership educator Sylvia Damiano and her work on how an understanding of the brain is affecting creativity, performance and leadership. Sylvia's work on neuro-leadership is compelling. As you may expect, a video from Sylvia can be watched on the *Amplifiers* website, along with links to her work. Simply go to www.amplifiersthebook.com and click on 'videos'.

In their book, *Beyond Reason: Using Emotions as You Negotiate*, negotiation expert Roger Fisher and his co-author Daniel Shapiro suggest that working through emotions is critical to great negotiation. They suggest, however, that dealing with core underlying causes of the emotions will get you more successfully to a win/win yes, than directly battling the emotions themselves. This thinking correlates with best practice sales and influence strategies, all of which suggest that managing the critical next step of the conversation, and not getting caught up in the other side's emotions or objections, will keep the deal on track and lead to more successful results.

Fisher and Shapiro contend that all emotions are built on five core concerns. They are:

- appreciation

- affiliation

- autonomy

- status

- role.

You can see that each of these core concerns would be enough to push people into the red zone. People literally cannot see beyond their emotional fields. The point here is to see how what we feel inside of us affects what happens outside of us. If you are in the business of people and leadership then you just have to become a master at understanding the triggers and barriers that help or prevent people move forward.

I'll close off then with this final word from neuroanatomist and Oprah star guest Jill Bolte Taylor, author of *My Stroke of Insight: A Brain Scientist's Personal Journey*. You can watch Jill deliver a cracker of a presentation, unpacking the complex relationship between the logical and emotional hemispheres of the brain. To see Jill's fabulous presentation on her stroke and her subsequent observations, simply go to the *Amplifiers* website at www.amplifiersthebook.com and click on 'videos'.

> When we are being compassionate, we consider another's circumstance with love rather than judgement…To be compassionate is to move into the right here, right now with an open heart consciousness and a willingness to be supportive…

> Although many of us may think of ourselves as thinking creatures that feel, biologically we are feeling creatures that think.

What Jill refers to in the previous quote is the work of amplifiers, and if you want to know how to do it, then read on—you are ready for part II.

Part II

THE HOW

It's easy to say 'let's be motivating as leaders', but rarely do we get to explore how that looks day to day. For years I have had the desire to play the guitar, and finally this year I took it up and am in a world of pain: it's a whole new language. Leadership, day to day is like playing songs on a guitar—you put together chords in different ways to play different songs for different audiences. Amplifiers have a whole bag full of chords they can play that will shift the energy in a business and in the people who are responsible for making the business work. Identifying the chords is easy: playing them well takes some practice.

This section is your chord master: it looks at a range of things leaders can do to be more motivational, to create more inspiring cultures and to transform the way work can work for the better.

CHAPTER 3

Motivation versus manipulation

This book is about motivational leadership. It's about inspiring others and doing this in a way that is seriously amplified: not only doing it, but also doing it big and bold. Not only doing it big and bold, but also actively developing it in and around you. In effect, not only being a ripple in a pond, but creating lots of others who are doing the same. It's about not only being a motivational leader but also developing motivational leadership in others.

So where did all this motivation stuff begin?

Well, depending on how far back you go, you could suggest that we have had world leaders who did this well or badly as good examples. I imagine Genghis Khan and Chairman Mao were pretty good amplifiers; Christopher Columbus and Marco Polo must have used some good rhetoric to get people to believe in their crazy enterprises. We also certainly have some good information on speaking to influence from the ancient Roman school of public speaking in Rhodes during Cicero's time, but let's come forward a little closer to now.

The first modern era example of motivational leadership is in the teachings of Napoleon Hill in his classic Think and Grow Rich programs. His first book, *The Law of Success*, was published in 1928. Much of the material in that book ended up in his *Think and Grow*

Rich book. So we could say ideas about motivational leadership started formally about 100 years ago.

The story goes — though it might be untrue — that Napoleon Hill, the father of self-help and modern motivational speaking, was interested in messages that impacted others. His desire was to understand how you could use oration and writing to affect people's lives. Being a man of faith he chose preachers as his mentors and role models. In his day a preacher often ran his sermons from a travelling tent, like a circus. Each month they would roll into a town. Desperate for entertainment and as a way of keeping the faith, people would take the family out for a sermon or two.

Hill would follow the most successful preachers, hoping to find patterns in the sermons. His desire was to see which sermons resonated best with the congregation, and after a while he recognised 16 core messages that seemed to be the most effective. Upon identifying these, he took some time to validate his findings and repackage them in a secular way. Basically, he removed the Jesus from the stories and built what we now know as the 16 mindsets, unpacked in the all-time bestseller *Think and Grow Rich*. These sermons became the various chapters in his book and modules in his courses.

The Napoleon Hill Foundation website shares a slightly different story on where the ideas in the book came from, built on the narrative and relationship between Napoleon Hill and his patron, Andrew Carnegie. The foundation says his theories came from interviewing more than 500 successful people.

So what does this have to do with your leadership and job as an amplifier? Well, in all things leadership, we need to look at what works. It does not matter much what story you believe — did he track preachers or interview successful people? The point is that Hill's messages are great starting points for developing an understanding of how to motivate others. These key messages work. They are like the tuning forks used by piano tuners that make the right sound when you tap them, a sound that is pleasing to the ear.

The ends may or may not justify the means but one thing is true: if you need to change how you communicate so that it's easier for your audience to hear a message then that's what you need to do. In communication, the leader takes responsibility for adapting to the audience. If a kid won't clean their room when you ask them, try different ways of having the conversation. It's about behavioural flexibility. It's the same here with Napoleon Hill's messages — they get the motivation job done. Get good at treating them less like laws and more like themes.

These themes act as hosts for your ideas. An idea that rocks will be shared by others and become viral. Attach any message to, or surround it with, one of these themes and it is more likely to get through and be shared.

You can read Napoleon Hill's messages as tips on how to be more successful, but students of amplification — motivational leaders — read them as key message tones that will influence and direct behaviour positively. Speechwriters understand them as key hot buttons that motivate and inspire.

Here is the list of messages from Napoleon Hill's laws of success:

1 The law of the mastermind

2 A definite chief aim

3 Self-confidence

4 Habit of saving

5 Initiative and leadership

6 Imagination

7 Enthusiasm

8 Self-control

9 Doing more than paid for

10 A pleasing personality

11 Accurate thinking

12 Concentration

13 Co-operation

14 Profiting by failure

15 Tolerance

16 The golden rule.

Many people are republishing Hill's work and putting their own names on it alongside Dr Hill's, and the Napoleon Hill Foundation has released unedited copies on Amazon. A full explanation of the 16 laws is shared at the *Amplifiers* website, www.amplifiersthebook.com. Follow the links to the Napoleon Hill resources.

I have adapted five of these messages and unpacked them below to set them in a 21st century context. Study all 16, but, as an amplifier, get used to working with these top five. These five message overtones become the end point in most amplifiers' conversations. The five main messages are:

1 *Desire.* The idea here is that everything begins by first developing a form of wanting among the people affected. Nothing happens unless someone wills or wishes it to be. Amplifiers will work hard to ensure that people want change, or desire growth. An amplifier will do the prep work of aligning desires and exploring desires. One technique that does this well is to simply ask questions such as, 'Is this something we want? How would this make things better or different?'

2 *Belief.* It follows that once a desire has been established or identified that belief is the next step. Desire is an internal attachment to something: desire is in the person. Belief is then a question around whether they think it's possible to get what they desire. If they want it and think it's possible, they are then required to ask questions that are less reflective and begin to take action.

3 *Focus.* If the person wants something and believes it's possible, the next button that needs to be pushed is the one of focus. Focus helps to narrow down options and prevent the huge feeling of overwhelm we get at the start of something new or different. The amplifier's job at this stage is to reduce the choices available. You don't have to dictate this restriction: you simply want to encourage people to reduce the options themselves.

4 *Commitment.* You will often see a leader make public declarations around what they plan to achieve. This is a technique that dances with the idea of commitment. Commitment is that step between the excitement of new and the harsh reality of what the individual needs to do. It's not only about the leader's promises, it's equally about the promises people make to themselves. Make sure you are including the sobering questions that drive commitment. When you have discussions around such questions as 'What might we have to give up?' 'What might we have to do differently?' 'What will we do if we hit some resistance on our way to our goal?' Here you are addressing commitment directly.

5 *Action.* Amplifiers have to be about action, performance and results. So it becomes critical that the final word for most conversations that motivational leaders have is on the subject of 'Do this!' Or 'What are you going to do?' Help people to focus on the few small actions they can take to get the ball rolling.

Here is how the five messages may look at the close of a speech. This shows them in action in one specific use—speaking. What follows is a made-up script. You can put your topic in the space provided and try this out next time you have to close a speech.

I guess, in closing, we need to realise that like most things in life [topic word] is only possible if you really want it. Today we are so overwhelmed with choice that we can have everything we want in life—just not all at the same time. You and I know that *desire* is not enough.

Whether what you heard today is new or something that is old, as if for the first time, it comes down to *belief.* Have we covered enough today for you to believe that this time things are going to be different?

But *belief* and *desire* don't mean you do anything. The difference between those who [insert the behavioural result you want] and those who don't is their degree of *commitment* to getting it.

Interested in something is *not* committed to it. [Insert personal story about something you have wanted to do for ages but are simply not committed enough to do anything about.]

So what you need to do is not get distracted by everything you need to do, but to just focus on the three things I shared with you today and nail them.

One thing that I know, having presented this message in one form or another for years to many people is that it is not the smartest or most talented people who get the best results.

It's those who take massive action towards their goal.

Whether it's in the motivational speaker context or a more intimate conversation, these themes are road-tested topics. Building the themes into your commutations will make them more motivational. Keep the top five as a checklist, and each time you have something to say, either to a group or one on one, think about how you can incorporate them to deliver your key ideas effectively.

The master manipulator

The German prefix *über* (the literal meaning is 'above') has crossed over into the English-speaking world, where it can have connotations of superiority, transcendence, excess or intensity, depending on the words with which it's combined. Typically *über* is used in conjunction with other words as a superlative. Many contemporary technology magazines and pop culture blogs use it to describe something as great. So I might call you an über-guru, or über-cool, for instance.

Friedrich Nietzsche, a fervent philosopher who was anti-democracy, anti-Christianity, anti-Judaism, anti-socialist and a self-proclaimed anti-Christ, expressed his belief in a master race and the coming of a superman in many of his works. His theory Übermensch described an elite group of super humans who were better than the rest — *mensch* being a word used to describe a member of the human race.

We know where this thinking led. Friedrich and his editor, his sister Elisabeth, were both anti-Semites, and the Nietzsches' philosophies were taken up by Hitler and influenced his horrific views, as published in *Mein Kampf*.

Hitler was a dark, twisted manipulator and by all accounts he was a motivator — a charming manipulator uses all the right tools for all the wrong reasons. He used various techniques and strategies to manipulate crowds in his public addresses to advance his agenda. He planted people in the audience whose job it was to 'stir'. They stood in the crowd and interacted with his speech, yelling out support for his ideas, cheering and starting 'spontaneous' applause. He is also reported to have used audio microphones and feedback loops to echo his voice and the audience response back onto the crowd, a known strategy for hyping up a mob of people.

I bring this up because in any discussion of motivational leadership with senior executive teams, the Hitler dimension usually comes up. This topic is usually raised as a question following any discussion around influence versus manipulation. The distinction is a troubling one for many.

The conversation usually becomes concerned with intent. Essentially the intent driving the amplifier is what draws the distinction between manipulation versus control. 'If my intent is clean,' one person will state, 'then it's influence. If my intent is not clean, then it is manipulation'.

It becomes a bit goodies versus baddies, and although the explanation sounds black and white, there are a few shades of grey.

The conversation often becomes heated and will typically divert, strangely, to the matter of gun control. Influence is compared to guns, one side of the room saying 'guns don't kill people, people kill people'. Others argue that the presence of guns is the root of the problem. The conversation then winds up in a right to bear arms and freedom of speech debate, and then it's time for doughnuts.

Aaron Sorkin, writer, director and mastermind behind the brilliant television series *The West Wing*, discussed the challenge of democracy in his movie *The American President*. Fictional US president Andrew Shepherd says in a press conference:

> America isn't easy. America is advanced citizenship. You've gotta want it bad, 'cause it's gonna put up a fight. It's gonna say, 'You want free speech? Let's see you acknowledge a man whose words make your blood boil, who's standing center stage and advocating at the top of his lungs that which you would spend a lifetime opposing at the top of yours.' Now show me that, defend that, celebrate that in your classrooms.
>
> Then you can stand up and sing about the land of the free.

It's been said that the sign of an advanced mind is the ability to handle ambiguity, contradiction and paradox. No doubt the intent to influence is a serious idea and one that in the right hands is powerful, and in the wrong hands—well, it's equally powerful. This is not a book on ethics or morality; this is not a book exploring whether your intent is good or bad: it's a book on motivation. In essence, it's a gun manual.

The intent to influence: seven guiding principles

These seven guiding principles for the intent to influence are, I believe, the seven things that need to be monitored with advanced leadership to ensure we have an intent to influence rather than a need to manipulate:

- It's about service, not ego.
- It's about inclusiveness, not exclusiveness.
- It's about diversity, not uniformity.
- It's about freedom, not control.
- It's about momentum, not inertia.
- It's about courage, not fear.
- It's about love, not hate.

If you put one group down in order to elevate yours, then you are on a slippery slope as a leader. If sarcasm is the lowest form of wit, because it is humour that occurs at the expense of another, then building yourself and your team up by putting others down is the lowest form of leadership.

Amplifiers lift the game, stay on the high ground and focus on results, not on talk. They come from love, not hate; they are building the world, not breaking it down. The intent is to influence and make the world better for all, not better for some. Amplifiers are generous, and, whether consciously or not, ask of themselves 'Does this come from love?' before they speak or act.

CHAPTER 4

The essence of amplification

The amplifier's journey begins with the acceptance of the job description of 'motivational leader'. It's about so much more, of course. Being a motivational leader is about understanding not only how motivation works but also the nature of inspirational leadership and how you go about orchestrating transformation. The unifying thread to the three ideas of motivation, inspiration and transformation, is most definitely the expectation of greatness.

Becoming an amplifier is about each leader realising that they can't simply deal with the left-brain logical, strategic initiatives of a business and call themselves a 'leader'. It's about inspiring people around you to create magic and to reach further than they thought they could. It's about leaders being all they can as a person. This is a confronting notion for some leaders, as it requires them to not only 'turn up' authentically as a human being but also to 'turn it up'.

If traditional leadership is about strategy, then motivational leadership is about using culture as a driver for strategy. If traditional leadership is about logic and analysis, then motivational leadership is about taking the decisions created through sound analysis and bringing these decisions all to life through emotions and engagement. If traditional leadership is about accountability and execution, then motivational leadership is about sustained effort and incredible performance. The leadership shift shown in figure 4.1 (overleaf) shows this change in how business is conducted.

Figure 4.1: the leadership shift

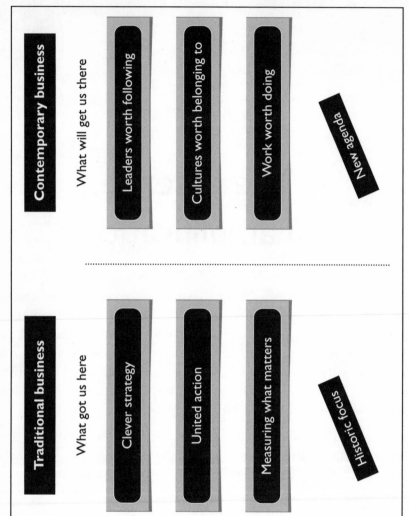

There is a synergistic play between traditional leadership and motivational leadership. This book is about 'and also', not 'either or'. It's about how motivational leadership takes the traditional leadership agenda and brings it alive and actually multiplies it.

Amplification answers the question 'Do we matter?', both for you as the motivational leader and for the people around you. Are you having an impact? Are you making a difference? The enemy of the amplifier is inactivity: amplifiers overcome inertia and get people moving. Amplifiers develop an obsessive focus on results.

Ross Williams is an entrepreneur and the business leader of a top-performing sales team in a New Zealand insurance company called Crombie Lockwood. He and his team are responsible for generating millions of dollars of new business each year. They are consistent top performers year in, year out, whether markets are tough or buoyant. He is without a shadow of a doubt an amplifier: he talks one on one and one to many, continuously activating the best in and for his team.

His daily mantra is 'Look at the scoreboard!' He uses this to focus his team on results. If he is ever faced with critics or strategy-obsessed players, he simply turns their attention to the results his people are delivering. Without an obsession with results, his amplification would be just talk.

Constant adherence to the scoreboard makes amplifiers meaningful; without some kind of change to the existing condition amplification becomes noise. This chapter explores the essence of amplification; specifically, how to go about bringing more motivation, inspiration and transformation into your life, business or community.

The three domains

Amplification requires a focus on three complementary domains: culture, work and leaders. The role of the amplifier is to help establish work worth doing, cultures worth belonging to and leaders worth following. These three areas of focus are complementary and synergistic.

The three pivotal actions are establishing *meaning* and *motivation* so that you can drive *results*. These are the daily to-dos for amplifiers. These actions are Business 101; the challenge is not knowing what to do (these three actions), but actually making it happen. Under each word on this model lies a whole gamut of theories and practices that will drive success for the leader and for the business.

Exploring the platforms

Figure 4.2 presents the thought-leading enterprise diagrammatically. The three platforms of work (work worth doing), culture (worth belonging to) and leaders (worth following) are fundamental to understanding how amplification operates.

First platform: the work—work worth doing

Average work is not very motivational. Work is essential and most of us have to do it, but let's face it, it is often pretty uninspiring. Even the most passionate individual who loves what they do still has moments where work just isn't working for them. The trick to creating work worth doing is not to make *all* the work worth doing. Larry Winget, author of *It's Called Work for a Reason*, has some pretty direct views on what work is and what it isn't.

> When everyone works half the time, it takes twice as many people to do the work. That translates to higher payroll expenses, higher insurance costs, higher taxes, and higher prices. The high cost of doing business is the result of lazy people not working. Reality check: It's called work for a reason! It's not called playtime. It's not called socializing time. It's called work. Sadly, most employees don't seem to understand this concept. Schools don't teach it. Kids aren't taught it at home. It isn't made clear to new employees.

Figure 4.2: the thought-leading enterprise

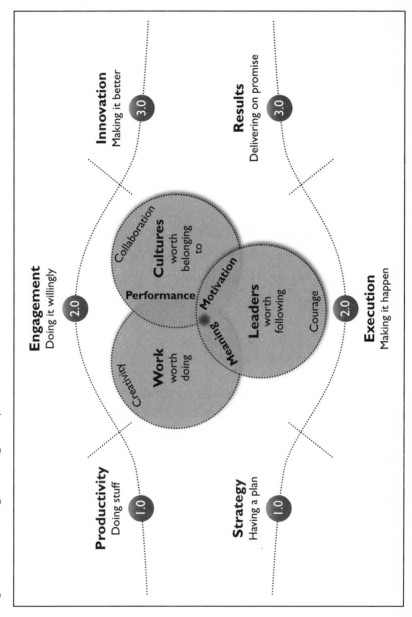

Love what he says and how he says it! The point of motivational leadership is not to make the work *all* good *all* the time, but rather to ensure that everyone gets moments of creativity, moments where they get to lose themselves in work — to be in flow. That delightful state at the edge of challenge and competency is described in peak performance researcher Mihaly Csikszentmihalyi's great work on high performance and is documented in his book *Flow: The Psychology of Optimal Experience*:

> People who have survived concentration camps or who have lived through near-fatal physical dangers often recall that in the midst of their ordeal they experienced extraordinarily rich epiphanies in response to such simple events as hearing the song of a bird in the forest, completing a hard task, or sharing a crust of bread with a friend.

He goes on to say 'The best moments usually occur when a person's body or mind is stretched to its limits in a voluntary effort to accomplish something difficult and worthwhile'. From his work and findings on the idea of the 'optimal experience' or being in the flow, he has concluded that it is something that we make happen: it lies at the intersection of what we can do and more than we thought we could do.

So it's about getting the right mix between challenge and capability. Nail this and we thrive at work; get it wrong and work becomes a grind. Challenge is about being stretched and capability is about feeling confident we can do the actual work required.

Second platform: the culture — culture worth belonging to

There is a saying that 'There are two types of couples in the world, those that fight all the time and those you don't know very well'. It's the same with cultures: the family cultures, the social cultures, our community cultures and, of course, our organisational cultures. A culture is the sum total of all the individuals that exist in it, and as a result cultures are not simple — but then I've never met a person who wasn't complex. So putting lots of individuals together isn't exactly going to be easy. Michael Henderson, anthropologist and author of more than seven books on culture, including *Get Tribal*, has this idea about culture to add to the idea of leaders worth following:

> A leader worth following is one who embodies the ideals and values of the tribe's culture. A leader who is able and willing to tell the tribe's stories regularly and with conviction, thus enabling the people to be reminded who they are. A leader worth following takes a deep and ongoing interest in the wellbeing of the people. The leader knows the culture, and sees culture as the key to weaving the people together.

In *Good to Great*, management consultant Jim Collins offers a functional view of the leader's role in getting the culture right. He believes getting the culture right is about getting the right people, on the right bus, in the right seats, heading in the right direction. Cultures worth belonging to are cultures that create shared experiences and enrich our lives. They are cultures that give us that sense of belonging, and they help us meet our core human drives. There are many models on human needs from the classic, such as Maslow's hierarchy of needs, through to the contemporary, such as Stephen Covey's four primary needs, through to the current ideas that business commentator Daniel H. Pink explores in his book *Drive: The Surprising Truth About What Motivates Us*.

Regardless of which model of human behavioural drivers you subscribe to, in its essence a great culture helps us live better, relate to others better, and grow and learn through the community, and gives us a chance to give back or make a difference.

Cultures give us something to do, someone to care about and something to hope for.

Third platform: the leader—leaders worth following

The third platform and the primary focus for this book is how to activate leadership throughout the family, community or business. It's about individuals stepping up and stepping out at all levels in the business. In the worldview through which I write this book, I feel that having groups, communities and businesses that are 'leaderful' is the smartest business strategy around.

Barry Posner and James Kouzes, leadership consultants, in their great book *The Truth About Leadership* state:

> You make a difference. Everything you will ever do as a leader is based on one audacious assumption. It's the assumption that you matter. Before you can lead others you have to lead yourself and believe that you can have a positive impact on others. You have to believe that your words can inspire and your actions can move others. You have to believe that what you do counts for something. If you don't, you won't even try. Leadership begins with you.

The best leaders bring out the greatness in the people around them and never stop doing so. The difficulty in leadership work lies in the impermanence of the results: just when you think you are done you have to start again. Much like painting a bridge, the maintenance is non-stop. The role and function of the motivational leader, then, is a job without end. It does not have an empty inbox, and any spare minute you have left after the functional doing of your job is then allocated to amplification.

There are many other great books on leadership, but for me *The 8th Habit: From Effectiveness to Greatness* by Stephen Covey is the best in compulsory reading texts. Not for its epiphany or extraordinary insight, but rather for its focus on the character of a leader, and getting from efficiency to greatness. Peter Hislop, an extraordinary executive leadership coach, believes that it's this 'expectation of greatness' that defines a leader. He contends that the main game is an expectation of yourself, of the people around you and indeed of the organisation as a whole that 'Great work will be done here'.

As figure 4.2 shows (see p. 49), there is a logical flow from first identifying strategy (1.0) to being able to execute (2.0) that strategy in a way that drives results (3.0). Sequence is critical. Initiatives are often deployed out of sequence, but leaders and cultures need to learn to walk before they can run. The first order of business is to get the group productive (1.0), then to focus on team engagement (2.0) before getting obsessed about innovation (3.0).

Too often innovation and results become the focus, when they are actually the goal. It's like four years of training as an Olympian — the gold medal is the goal, but it's not what the athlete focuses on during the 1460 days between Olympic Games. The athlete needs to work on the critical next actions that will take them to their goal. The swimmer swims; the runner runs. Sure, they keep glancing at the goal, but obsessing about the goal is not actually the key to getting better or achieving the goal.

It's well documented that any attempt to build an innovation pipeline in an organisation is about having a culture that's ready for innovation. Organisational structures have to match the initiative. The same is true for results-obsessed businesses: the action is to execute on strategy—the outcome will be the desired results.

Imagine a culture with poor engagement trying to deploy an innovation development program. If employee engagement is low, and employees don't like their work, then the company culture is disenfranchised and cynical. The language becomes, 'Why would I share my good idea if my boss is going to steal it and make out it was theirs? I am not sharing'. As a result innovation is dead in the water before it's even begun. This makes the case for the synergistic relationship between leadership, work and culture. You can't work on one and ignore the rest.

Triangles and circles

Culture is a complex, organic beast: it is not something you can legislate. You can't demand the elements of culture such as 'Have fun now!' or 'Like your co-worker today' or 'Work back late because this matters to us'. These things *may* happen when the culture allows it, but they can't be imposed. However, there are certain frameworks that make cultural initiatives work for you or against you.

An introduction to culture for amplifiers starts with understanding the play between command and control versus surrender and let go. Chris Anderson, senior editor of the magazine *Wired* and author of *Free: How Today's Smartest Businesses Profit by Giving Something for Nothing*, named it well in his opening piece on the changing landscape of business. He juxtaposed two dynamics—scarcity and abundance—that he believes new business needs to consider (see table 4.1, overleaf).

Table 4.1: the changing business landscape

	Scarcity	**Abundance**
Social model	Paternalism (We know best)	Egalitarianism (You know best)
Decision process	Top down	Bottom up
Rules	Everything is **forbidden** unless it is permitted	Everything is **permitted** unless it is forbidden
Management style	Command control	Out of control
Profit plan	Business model	Make it up as we go along

The shift in approach, this changing business landscape, is one you can express geometrically without too much discussion. Sit a bunch of your people around and draw two shapes, a triangle and a circle. Then ask the group to choose which shape best fits their current business, then their department, then their role. Then ask them to feel free to reshape their shape; maybe it's a triangle with rounded edges. Finally ask the group what they believe the shape needs to be and why. The discussions from these two dynamics are very instructive.

The triangle represents command and control, and resource management. The leadership is most definitely top down in a triangle. For people who have been brought up within a hierarchical religious worldview, having God at the top of the pyramid, priests a little lower down and then people at the bottom, this is a comfortable perspective. It is also the traditional feudal model and the military model for many who serve in the armed forces. To paraphrase the famous line from the Tennyson poem *The Charge of the Light Brigade*, 'Ours is not to reason why. Ours is but to do and die', says it all.

To be perfectly clear, I think triangles rock. Triangles very quickly marshal a set of resources and get things done. The back end of my consulting practice runs like a triangle. I make stuff up; a team member sets things up; and another cleans things up. We all happily process huge amounts of stuff, as we stay focused on our functional roles.

In my opinion triangle cultures really come into their own in life or death situations. Most surgeons run a triangle structure when operating, and I'm glad about it. I don't want a whole heap of brainstorming going on during brain surgery. The fire brigade also operates in a command and control structure. Just as well — if my house is burning I don't want some kind of team building love-in getting in the way of saving my house, or a loved one.

Triangles work well and have done so for centuries. However, some initiatives just don't work very well in command and control environments. A consultative leadership style is not going to work in triangle formation. A request for innovative ideas across the firm is not going to work. As a leader, you need to match the initiatives to the cultural dynamic at play.

The circle, on the other hand, represents a flatter, more open organisational structure. The leader is at the centre of a set of concentric circles. Circle businesses tend to be more creative, open plan and risk taking than triangle ones. Typically they are leaner operations and gaining access to senior leadership is very easy. The culture is quite informal and inclusive, and people truly are empowered to get things done in the best possible way. Groups form and break down quite organically. Creative teams work on projects, quite often recruiting talent from within the business and wooing them away from other projects they have been working on.

The software game design company Valve is the modern poster child for the circle structure. Their employee induction manual is a cracker of a read — you can download the manual from the *Amplifier* website. Simply go to www.amplifiersthebook.com and click on 'Extras'.

Here is an extract from that manual. Thanks to my mate and fabulous expert on Making Clever Happen, Dr Jason Fox, for sharing.

Welcome to Flatland

Hierarchy is great for maintaining predictability and repeatability. It simplifies planning and makes it easier to control a large group of people from the top down, which is why military organisations rely on it so heavily.

But when you're an entertainment company that's spent the last decade going out of its way to recruit the most intelligent, innovative, talented people on Earth, telling them to sit at a desk and do what they're told obliterates 99 percent of their value.

They then go onto explain that they want innovators to work for them and want to ensure that people feel empowered to do great work rather than worry about reporting into someone above them in the business organisation chart. The founders of Valve believe that a flat structure will remove many of the barriers that exist in businesses and that get in the way of everyone in the business getting closer to the customer.

There is an interesting discussion in the manual about the huge responsibility that goes into flattening a business. Employees are empowered and at the same time they need to take personal responsibility for what they do. There are no excuses or 'passing the buck' to someone else in the business. It's for this reason that the team at Valve obsess about hiring. They ask the question when interviewing candidates, 'are they talented?' and 'are they innovative' they also ask 'could this person run the company?' because in a way everyone who works at Valve does.

The classic MBA case study of a circle or flat organisation is the company W. L. Gore & Associates, famous for making cool jackets in their proprietary fabric Gore-Tex. It has also innovated into aerospace, medical and so many other unexpected places, producing market-leading guitar strings, dental floss, fuel cells, cardiovascular and surgical applications and all kinds of specialised fabrics. The owners run their business very flat, with as little command structure as possible. This, they say, has led to hugely profitable adaptations and applications for their core products, as employees are given incentives to take ideas and run with them.

Bill Gore set up the company with his wife Genevieve in the family garage in 1958. He wanted to build a firm that was truly innovative and had no rule books and no bureaucracy. It was his belief that people come to work to do well and to do the right thing.

Journalist Simon Caulkin interviewed the CEO Terri Kelly for *The Observer* in 2008. He reported that 'trust, peer pressure and the desire to invent great products...would be the glue holding the company together, rather than the official procedures other companies rely on.'

Terri Kelly relied on the unofficial procedures and lack of hierarchy at W.L. Gore and Associates when she turned down Bill's request to look after a pet project when she was just a young engineer with the company. She went on to become the president and chief executive in 2005. Leaders are not appointed at Gore, they emerge when they accumulate enough followers to qualify them. As the interview reveals, 'Although there is a structure (divisions, business units and so on) there is no organisation chart, no hierarchy and therefore no bosses.' Terry Kelly is one of the few employees with a title and 'it works just fine,' she says. In fact her views on the financial crisis directly relate it to management crisis and the symptom of a wider issue: a deficit of trust. Simon Caulkin writes:

> Counter-intuitively, the best governance, especially in troubled periods, is the absence of external rules: Gore would rather rely on fiercely motivated people who, having internalised true north, have no fear of challenging leaders to justify decisions, and leaders who know they can't rely on power or status to get themselves out of a fix.

The triangle and circle conversation is a fascinating one to have with senior leaders, strategic thinkers and department heads in your business. Amplification works very well in both triangles and circles, as well as in hybrids. The approach when amplifying the culture in each is different, but the role and function are the same.

CHAPTER 5

Talking heads

The movie *Cool Hand Luke* has a famous line, spoken by Strother Martin acting as the captain (prison warden) after beating the hero, Luke, in front of a prison chain gang: 'What we've got here is a failure to communicate.' Often it feels that leadership communication, whether it's in the home or the boardroom, is a colossal failure to communicate. We want it to be a meeting of the minds but instead we end up with, at best, a lot of talk that goes nowhere and at worst a complete breakdown between intent and what gets said.

Amplification is about leadership, and a huge part of that is the quality of the communication a leader creates in and around their world.

The three golden rules

Whenever you are sharing an idea as an amplifier, whether it's in a bedroom presentation or a ballroom presentation, you need to keep the three major rules of communication front of mind.

Rule 1: You don't matter.

Rule 2: They don't care.

Rule 3: They're not listening.

Can you believe I make a living as a motivational speaker?

The tools in this book explore how you can be an amplifier and turn up the amount of motivational and inspirational leadership in and around you. It's critical, though, that before we launch into any of the 'how and what' of amplification that you keep these three golden rules front and centre. These become the filters you run your words, conversations and ideas through.

They bear repeating: you don't matter; they don't care; and they're not listening.

Here's how they work.

It's not *really* that you don't matter, but more that focusing on yourself sets the whole relationship with your audience, the team at work, or your family, off on the wrong foot. The first step is to get out of you and into the world of the people you are addressing. If you are nervous in any way, it's because your attention is focused inwards, on what's going on inside of you. Switch and focus your attention outwards. This simple flip in your attention can help you overcome nerves, and get your head in the right space prior to any leadership based communication.

It's not *really* that they don't care but more that they won't care until you have given them a reason to care. The price of entry into any relationship is relevance. How is what you are about to say important, urgent and relevant to your audience? Too many people launch into content-based communication without first establishing an agreed reason for caring about the content. Sell me on why before you start to explain what or how.

It's not *really* that they are not listening directly, but rather that you are speaking a different language. Take some time to learn the different listening languages people use. Are they detail thinkers or big picture thinkers? Are they analytical or creative? Are they visual or auditory? Do they want things organised simply or do they care more about distinctions and discussion? As a leader you need to develop the behavioural flexibility to connect with different people differently.

Four critical actions

The four critical actions that address the three rules for better communication are:

- Think before you speak.

- Speak their language.

- Frame things for understanding.

- Drive for action—because amplifiers have a bias towards action and a requirement to make it more than talk, this fourth point focuses on a shift, a change and some kind of movement.

Think before you speak

One of my early books, *Thought Leaders: How to Capture, Package and Deliver your Ideas for Greater Commercial Success*, explores how to unpack what you know in great detail. There are essentially three problems with how people go about preparing to communicate: they may have half-baked ideas, self-centred thinking or their thinking may be out of whack. Table 5.1 shows the relationship between the challenges we all face, the keys to overcoming them and then some specific techniques amplifiers use to get over this stage and progress things. (The techniques suggested in this and the following tables are all discussed in more detail later in this chapter.)

Table 5.1: think before you speak

Points of failure	Keys to overcoming	Techniques to use
Half-baked ideas	Think before you speak	1: Full spectrum thinking
Self-centred thinking	Know what's important to them	2: Clicking process
Your thinking is out of whack	Own your stuff	3: Identify cognitive distortions

Speak their language

We often communicate with others through our personal preferences and miss the fact that communication is only as good as the other person's understanding. You can talk as much as you like, but if the message is not getting through, then you have a failure to communicate. There are three problems going on between you and the receiver: you don't think before you speak; you have no idea of or are ignoring their listening language; you don't repeat what you say often enough for them.

Amplifiers, however, will develop extreme behavioural flexibility to get their point across in the best way possible. Table 5.2 shows the relationship between the challenges you face in communicating, the keys to overcoming those challenges, and some specific techniques amplifiers use to discover how to speak their audience's language and progress things.

Table 5.2: speak their language

Points of failure	Keys to overcoming	Techniques to use
You ignore their language	Speak the way they listen	4: Nine learning channels
You don't repeat what you say	Repetitive variety	5: Linguistic palette
You miss the mark	Pitch it at the right level	6: World views

Frame things for understanding

You can do a lot to help people hear your message more effectively, by understanding that you need to prepare people to receive your message. Rather than simply blurting out your perspective, you must take the time to plan for success. This is necessary sometimes because people listen through their bias; they dismiss through personality; and are often stuck in emotions, and as an amplifier you need to be able to break through those barriers. Table 5.3 shows the relationship between the challenges you face, the keys to overcoming them and then some specific techniques amplifiers use to get over this stage and progress things.

Table 5.3: frame things for understanding

Points of failure	Keys to overcoming	Techniques to use
They hear through bias	Frame out problems	7: Use the 15 questions
They dismiss through personality	Behavioural flexibility	8: Personality awareness
They are stuck in emotions	Identify cognitive distortions	9: Stay on the critical path

Drive for action

I keep harping on the point that amplifiers need to be results obsessed. Achieving results is the Achilles heel of amplification—too much talk, not enough action. So in all things you do as an amplifier you need to ask the question 'Are we making a difference?' People get lost in their priorities; they often lack the know-how and get stuck in inertia. Table 5.4 shows the relationship between the challenges you face, the keys to overcoming them and then some specific techniques amplifiers use to get over this stage, take action and progress things.

Table 5.4: drive for action

Points of failure	Keys to overcoming	Technique
Lost in priorities	Lay it out	10: First things first
Lack the know how	Share the way	11: Why to if
Stuck in inertia	Get people moving	12: The nine integrations

The 12 techniques in focus

The 12 techniques discussed in these four steps (the right-hand columns in the previous tables) are worthy of a book in their own right. When we run leadership development programs we explore each in turn and help leaders use them in their day-to-day functions and roles. Here I provide a quick high-level explanation of each; some are proprietary techniques used in our consulting business Thought Leaders Global, and some are the work of other subject matter experts (some are discussed further later in this book). You can find out more about Thought Leaders and what we do at www.thoughtleadersglobal.com.

1: Full spectrum thinking

Ideas are big picture and detailed, analytical and emotional. These four concepts sit like the north (N), south (S), east (E) and west (W) of an idea. When you communicate as a leader you make sure you have communicated your idea with enough depth and breadth that it's a complete and whole idea. The big picture may be communicated with metaphors or contextual models; the detail may be communicated with case studies or great storytelling.

As a leader you have four roles that follow this way of thinking about ideas, you have to paint a picture of the future (NW); you have to join the dots between one idea and the next (SW); you have to share ways for getting things done (SE); and you have to be able to bring it all alive (NE) for the people around you.

2: Clicking process

This is essentially an empathy process that shows you how to communicate to others, starting from their needs, not your awareness. When you know a lot about your chosen topic you tend to be further along the journey of understanding than your listener, or reader. As a result you often miss the essential communication piece of meeting people where they live.

Great marketers and salespeople tend to win business not so much because of what they know but rather because of the way they are able to communicate what they know in a way that appears relevant to the other party. They kind of click their goal, idea or objective with the listeners' real-world concerns.

To click well with someone else, you want to start by empathically and compassionately connecting with the challenges or aspirations that are front-of-mind for them. You want to have a gentle conversation around the challenges or aspirations they are facing in their world.

Once you have compassionately established and agreed on what are the big priority challenges being faced by the other person, it's time to shift energy and demonstrate your knowledge of the subject. This is a shift from compassion to expertise. It helps to draw diagrams on napkins, coasters or whiteboards in this second step in the clicking process.

The final step, following on from first compassionately connecting to their issues and unpacking some ideas on why that may be is to present with conviction a clear and confident series of next steps.

3: Identify cognitive distortions

Cognitive distortions are simply ways that our mind convinces us of something that isn't really true. These inaccurate thoughts are usually used to reinforce negative thinking or emotions—telling ourselves things that sound rational and accurate, but really only serve to keep us feeling bad about ourselves.

Cognitive distortions are simply ways that the mind can convince us of something that isn't true. Our minds then usually build negative self-talk around these events and we then experience unhelpful emotions. Both camps agree that the distortions are valid and true; they disagree on how to manage them. Great leaders know that these ways of thinking are not what we want to amplify.

Leading psychotherapist Aaron Beck, in his book *Cognitive Therapies*, introduced the theory of cognitive distortions, and psychotherapist David Burns, in his book *Feeling Good: The New Mood Therapy*, popularised the theory.

For the amplifier, the trick to managing cognitive distortion is not to conduct pop psychology of your team, but rather to be able to recognise these unhelpful thought processes in both yourself and others. Realising that your thinking may be out of whack is the first step to doing something about it.

Practitioners of cognitive behaviour therapy (CBT) believe that by refuting the negative thinking over and over again, the problem will slowly diminish over time and be automatically replaced by more rational and balanced thinking. Over the 30 years or so since the work of Beck and Burns, we have seen a splintering in thought between those who believe this to be true and those who suggest quite adamantly that the exact opposite is the case—that by taking your negative thoughts seriously you are actually preventing the success that CBT is trying to achieve.

More recently the approach of those trained to help people with how they think has shifted towards a new model of treatment. The acceptance and commitment therapy (ACT) group believe you should accept the negative thoughts and acknowledge them for what they are, but instead of refuting and working on them, you take action in spite of them. Leading sports psychologist Michael Martin says 'it's about not taking negative thoughts seriously'.

Both groups of therapists agree that the distortions are valid and true, but they disagree on how to manage them. Great leaders know that the following ways of thinking are not what we want to amplify. The common cognitive distortions are:

- *Filtering.* You don't see any good in a situation: instead, you filter out the good stuff.

- *Polarised, or black and white, thinking.* As the name suggests, this is a thinking state where we see things only as either good or bad. There is little room for the necessary grey areas that life situations exhibit.

- *Overgeneralisation.* This is the simplifying of life down to a standard of all-encompassing rule. A 'this always happens to me' way of seeing the world.

- *Jumping to conclusions.* This is the dangerous act of making people's minds up for them and assuming we know what they are saying before they have had a chance to communicate.

- *Catastrophising.* This is the act of living in drama: everything is perceived as bigger than it is, and worse than it is. This cognitive distortion is often a function of perfectionism.

- *Personalisation.* This is the ultimate in taking things personally. Every problem and bad event could be prevented if the person were not so...[something].

Other cognitive distortions include control and control and fairness fallacies, blaming, the continuous use of 'should' (having a set of rules about how people *should* behave), emotional reasoning, global labelling (generalising qualities to create a negative judgement), and the need to always be right.

For leaders, being vigilant for detecting these ways of thinking personally means you are coming from the right place when you amplify. A rudimentary knowledge of them also helps you coach others with their thinking—not to pretend some skill in therapy, but simply to know what is helpful thinking and what is not.

4: Nine learning channels

Howard Gardner, a development psychologist from Harvard University, describes what he calls 'Minds for now and minds for the future'. The nine most common minds or ways of thinking he describes are incredibly useful for leaders—these information processing ways of thinking are like people's preferred TV channels. Gardner's work has led to a revolution in teaching styles, in which the teacher adapts to the classroom's learning needs. This is a sharp contrast with the traditional teaching model, in which the student does all the adapting.

The *Amplifiers* website at www.amplifiersthebook.com has more detail and graphics on all these techniques.

This focus on learning channels, thinking models or information processing modes can be organised into three levels, each with three focuses or channels. The first level is all about learning or hearing something for the first time; the second is all about arranging information that you are already familiar with; and the third and final level is used for organising information that you are quite knowledgeable about.

In the first level, the first three focuses are to do with learning things for the first time. They are visual, auditory and kinesthetic. Visual is all about 'show me', auditory is all about 'tell me' and kinesthetic is all about 'let me'. We all use all of these channels at different times. The sensory focus of these first three channels makes them better ways of processing information when learning something new. We go into sensory overload when hearing things for the first time.

The three channels in the second level of learning are to do with arranging ideas in our mind: they are the perfect information processing channels if you are talking to someone who has a good idea of the topic you are discussing. The three intermediate channels are numeric, linguistic and interpersonal. Numeric is all about lists and order; linguistic is all about language and meaning; and interpersonal is all about examples that embed the information.

The last three channels in the third level are the ways that experts may process new information on a topic they have studied for some time. They are abstract, existential and intrapersonal. Abstract is all about 'what's this like?' and the need for references; existential is focused on 'what's this about?', and so seeks to understand the big picture themes you are sharing; and intrapersonal is about the age-old question 'what's in it for me?'

Understanding that not all people listen and learn in the same way that you do is essential to getting more people on board. Amplifiers need to know their strengths and weaknesses across these main different thinking, learning and information processing channels.

5: Linguistic palette

This is a simple thinking and planning process that essentially increases a leader's vocabulary around key messages. It explores ways in which you can say the same thing lots of different ways. It is taken from Speakership, one of our public speaking programs for senior organisational leaders.

If flexibility is the key to effective leadership communication, then having access to a variety of ways of expressing your point is critical; learning expert Glenn Capelli says it's about 'repetitive variety'.

The two basic linguistic palettes we can adopt as amplifiers are the formal and the casual palette. At a minimum, be sure to have these two ways of making a point. I may say 'sex is good' or 'fornication benefits all': one is expressed casually, the other formally.

Increasing your available options to make a point is smart — essentially you get to think once and use often. Beyond the formal and the casual palettes you may want to plan four other linguistic palettes. Make your point so it's simple (1), so it's inspiring (2), so it's practical (3), and so it's sagacious (4). We call this the generational palette process: speak so a 7-year-old would understand your message (simple); so a 17-year-old would listen to it (inspirational); so a 37-year-old would pay attention (practical); and so a 70-year-old would value it (sagacious).

6: World views

Drawn from work by corporate anthropologists Michael and Shah Henderson in their great book *Leading Through Values*, this process seeks to understand a leader's predominant world view with the aim of developing an understanding of what to say, when and to whom.

Imagine explaining species extinction to a poacher in Africa. The poacher knows that by hunting and killing a white rhino they get to feed their family for a year. The rhino's plight in the wider planetary vision is too far removed from their world view. You can only ever argue with someone to the level of their perspective.

The Hendersons unpack five primary world views: survival, institutional, self-actualised, collaborative and symbiotic. If you lay these out in a line there is a kind of ascension from simply trying to get by, through to realising that we are all connected. This work parallels the work of Don Beck (an authority on values systems) and Clare Graves (the company founder of Spiral Dynamics) with *Spiral Dynamics* and the earlier work of psychologist Abraham Maslow in his theory of human motivation and model of the hierarchy of needs.

Amplifiers meet people where they live and match their thinking, and then pace the communication so that it is first understood at the level of perception or world view of the main audience. Then the conversation, often over time, evolves onto progressive world views that are more productive.

7: Use the 15 questions

Explored in part III of this book, these questions become framing strategies. A framing strategy is planning for the worst in your leadership communication. It's all about anticipating what may go wrong when you communicate in a particular environmental context. Taking the time to work through the questions and answering them will enable you to enrol key people to your thinking and reduce the friction of assumptions and mental blocks that will come up against what you are trying to achieve.

The questions are explored in a lot more detail in part III, but for now it's worth considering the five areas and concerns they address. The first set of questions is all about making what you are talking about a *priority*: you need to answer the questions of why this message, why now and why are you the person to be sharing it with? The second set of questions look into the theme of *positioning*: you want to explore the answers to questions such as who are you, what do you do and why should I care?

Once you have nailed these initial issues of priority and positioning and you have thought through how to capture the attention of your listeners, the next piece of work you need to do is a little subtler. You need to help your audience overcome their biases and snap judgements: you need to help them over the barriers—the subconscious questions that prevent them understanding you or listening to what you have to say. The barriers become what's wrong with you, what's wrong with them and what's wrong with your message? This set of questions is all about the superficial and realising that, as a leader, superficial is anything but. If you have a funny accent, if they are in a particular mood or your message is a little foreign to their mindset you need to knock over these barriers before you communicate anything.

Once the barriers are down, you need to make sure you have the smart cookies in the room totally switched on. These next three questions borrow from technique 4, the nine mindsets. Anyone with an advanced understanding of your message or topic needs to be enrolled before you launch into the main points in your communication. This process of enrolment begins with referencing your message, explaining it at its highest level and being absolutely clear what the pay off will be for people who listen or act on what you say. You need to answer the questions 'What's it like?', 'What's it about?' and 'What's in it for me?'

The final piece of work you do in framing out concerns is to focus on *action*. Essentially you have your audience's attention, the questions now are what's your point, how is it different and what do you want me to do now?

The thinking you create on the other side of hypothetically answering these questions gets you ready to rock when you communicate, no matter what may happen.

8: Personality awareness

All models are flawed and all models are useful, and when it comes to models on personality they all have definite strengths and weaknesses. This process skims over the various ways personality is identified and uses these techniques to help you develop behavioural flexibility.

Probably the oldest profiling tool on the planet is the Chinese I Ching concept that was explored in a classic Chinese text known as *The Book of Changes*. Basically this model of the world suggests that there are four primary domains: earth, fire, water and air. I Ching explores metal as a fifth element and space as a sixth. These domains are used to explain the seasons, establish when to plant crops and explain how to understand behaviour as well as a range of other applications from navigation to wealth creation. The I Ching is simply a model of the world, a way of seeing things. It does not have to be true or accurate really, it simply has to be useful.

Viewed from a personality or behaviours filter, people who are earth are very pragmatic; fire people are very inspirational; water people are relational; and air people are judgemental. Now, to be clear, we label jars not people. I have never met a person who wasn't complex and multifaceted. It is too simple to break people down into four or even six dimensions. The more you get to know someone the less powerful these tools become. You can, however, be aware of the needs someone has as a person when they are being earth, fire, water or air.

Essentially you need to know how you are being perceived and what the other person's needs are and, if there is a major mismatch, you as the amplifier need to use profiling as a tool only, and not as the truth.

9: Stay on the critical path

Perspective for the critical path—what needs to be done next—is a hugely valuable thinking process. This module looks at how to identify critical milestones, stay on path and manage the emotional sidetracks that get in the way. This process draws heavily on acceptance and commitment therapy and blends classical project management frameworks.

At its simplest, critical path thinking is about staying on track; the key directional questions that sit behind this process are, at the beginning of any next process, 'Is this the best use of our time right now?' and during a process 'What are we trying to decide here—what questions are we answering?' And finally, when making a decision at the end of a process, 'Will this get us closer to our goal or not, and what is our next step?'

10: First things first

Drawing on the work of Stephen Covey, leadership consultant and best-selling author, and his thinking around managing priorities, this is a simple process that helps you gain clarity around what to do next. It involves incorporating decision-making processes, forced ranking and many other simple techniques for keeping the main thing as the main thing.

Covey suggests a four-step framework for keeping the main things in your life front of mind. His premise is that we let urgency get in the way of the things that matter most. We get busy and caught up doing things, and forget to ask in all the busy-ness 'Is this what I want?' 'Is this what I chose?'

Covey describes four domains of activity organised around the two dimensions of urgency and importance, and he names them quadrant one through to quadrant four. Quadrant one activities are those things we have to do that are both urgent and important. Managers say that they spend most of their day putting out fires: this is quadrant one. Covey contests that we have so much of this in our life because we have not spent enough time on the quadrant two activities in our life. Quadrant two is all about those things that are important, but have no sense of urgency to them: for instance, exercise is never urgent yet we all know it's important. Planning is never urgent, but it sure helps prevent future chaos and stress. By making time for the activities that matter most before they become urgent we begin to gain some control over the personal chaos that affects most leaders. Knowing these activities and focusing people on the correct next things helps them from becoming lost in conflicting priorities. The third quadrant is all about managing other people so that their priorities don't become yours. Quadrant four is all about eliminating the time wasting when we operate and live by default and not by design.

11: Why to if

Building on the 4MAT model of Bernice McCarthy—a teacher famous for systemising class plans—this process helps you unpack any idea through a series of models and stages. The deeper we know a subject the harder it can be to communicate its value to others. This process addresses the gap between what the teacher knows and what the student cares about. The process is also super useful for leaders who need to get people on board to the business's vision.

This gets explored in more detail in part III, as a high level introduction there provides a sensible order for unpacking information. Essentially the process is around starting with *why* the message matters, then explaining *what* the message is and *how* people can implement it, and finishing the process by explaining the consequences of either doing or not doing, implementing or not implementing: understanding and applying this last step becomes about *if*.

Amplifiers use what works, what gets results. This process is a proven one that helps people know exactly what you are saying.

12: The nine integrations

Taken from the programs we run on productivity, this process unpacks the three actions, platforms and rest strategies for people wanting to become mega productive. Personal and team productivity are a required study for amplifiers. These nine integrations become a tool amplifiers can use to audit their capacity to get things done in and around them. If amplification is about driving results these nine integrations make it possible. An amplifier needs prodigious amounts of energy: there is a lot of heavy emotional lifting and a huge need to get out and on with it. You need a sound body, mind and soul. Let any one of these three spheres drop and you decrease your capacity to work.

These nine ideas are sequential coaching actions. If you find yourself helping one of your team to be productive, you can explore these nine integrations and identify opportunities to reduce the struggle and turn up their capacity to do more and be more. Personally, as an amplifier, you monitor these nine, ensuring you stay fully charged and able to do great work.

Once you get the three spheres of attention (body, mind and soul) dialled in, you want to go about working the plan that ensures each sphere is operating at its peak. You identify for each the key activities that develop them, you build platforms that ensure capacity within each sphere and then install strategies that allow you to recharge the battery for each sphere. These three spheres and the workout plan for each form are shown in figure 5.1.

Figure 5.1: the nine integrations

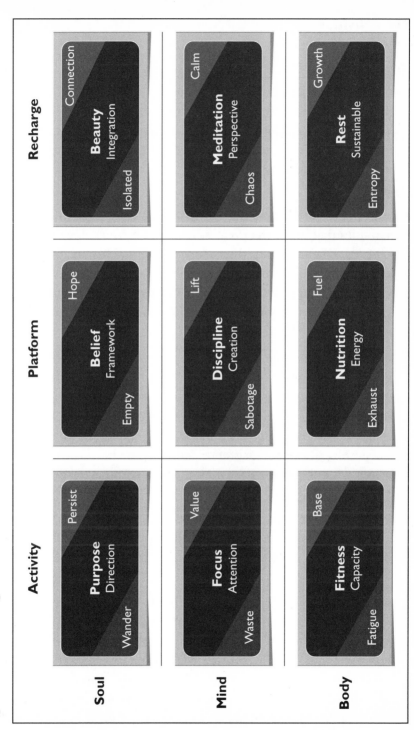

	Activity	**Platform**	**Recharge**
Soul	Persist / **Purpose** Direction / Wander	Hope / **Belief** Framework / Empty	Connection / **Beauty** Integration / Isolated
Mind	Value / **Focus** Attention / Waste	Lift / **Discipline** Creation / Sabotage	Calm / **Meditation** Perspective / Chaos
Body	Base / **Fitness** Capacity / Fatigue	Fuel / **Nutrition** Energy / Exhaust	Growth / **Rest** Sustainable / Entropy

The activities

The activities consist of fitness, focus (pay attention to what matters) and purpose (follow the through line).

- *Concentrate on fitness.* Fitness gives us the capacity to achieve so much in our lives. Amplifiers make building a base level of fitness a critical part of their leadership plan. Working on your fitness increases your capacity to work and enhances the quality of your work. Without it you fatigue easily and cannot realise your goals and ambitions.

- *Pay attention to what matters.* Amplifiers pay attention to the activities that bring the greatest reward. They manage distractions, keep their head and do the right next thing. This means that every minute or resource they have available is used in the most valuable way possible. Focus is the key to minimising waste. Don't multitask, stay on task, avoid the shiny objects and get the job done.

- *Follow the through line.* There is a line between where we are and where we want to be. Knowing your purpose allows you to walk that line. Having a clearly understood purpose gives you direction; without direction we are wandering in the forest of 'stuff'. Doing plenty of stuff, but not really going anywhere. Purpose is all about persistence: a clear sense of purpose helps the tough get going no matter how tough the going gets.

The platforms

The platforms consist of nutrition (rubbish in, rubbish out), discipline (do that thing) and belief (a view of the world).

- *Rubbish in, rubbish out.* Learn about food: it's the fuel for focus, productivity and so much more. If being fit gives you a capacity to work, great nutrition gives you the energy to work. Fitness is a long-term game: it's got huge amounts of delayed gratification in it. Food and nutrition—eating well has an immediate impact on how you think now and what you can do in a very short amount of time. Exercise for how you will feel tomorrow but eat for how you will feel in 30 minutes or three hours' time.

- *Do that thing.* Discipline is about doing the things you don't want to do. For many this becomes the big D word. The trick with discipline is to flip the switch. It's not about developing or focusing on the act of discipline (that's too punitive): it's about turning the tough tasks into acts of creation. If you ask yourself, 'What can I create today?' you will find an energetic lift pushing you to do, rather than some kind of emotional cattle prod. Without discipline we tend to sabotage ourselves and block our best interest.

- *A view of the world.* I want to be super careful not to suggest any kind of belief system in this final platform. It's been shown again and again that people who have a view of the world—a belief system—are better off than those who don't. It provides a framework for staying hopeful. The belief can be in a deity, a science or simply a model for being. It's not about the belief: it's about how having one gives your life fullness.

The recharge

Recharge consists of rest (plan laziness), meditation (burn a candle) and beauty (smell the sunsets).

- *Plan laziness.* One of the odd paradoxes with your body is that most of the fitness and wellbeing benefits are achieved after you work out and after you eat. It's the stopping that allows the body to enhance, upgrade and enrich itself. By being active then passive you maintain a sustainable growth. When you go, go, go all the time you end up encouraging more rapid entropy.

- *Burn a candle.* Meditation is all about stopping the noise for a bit, stepping back and achieving perspective. This helps you sit in the middle of the storm. Amplifiers are results focused and as such will find themselves in hurricanes of projects, people and ideas. You need to be able to find your calm in the chaos—meditation in all its forms helps with this.

- *Smell the sunsets.* The reward for a life of personal growth and transformation is a raw appreciation of beauty and art, both natural and human creations. When you appreciate beauty your soul achieves a higher level of integration. You feel connected to everyone and everything. This is why art transforms community and why we must be patrons of all that expresses the best in humanity. It's no surprise that artists become activists; it's no surprise that a community, a suburb or a commercial development is enhanced when artists find their way there.

These nine integrations help you get more done in less time and are foundational focuses for amplifiers. Now we get serious and move to part III for the heavy-duty amplifier development tools.

Part III

THE WHAT

The three goals of work worth doing, cultures worth belonging to and leaders worth following are true for profit-centred enterprises, not-for-profits, government bodies, volunteer communities, educational faculties and families. My partners and I at Thought Leaders Global think it's the alignment of these three goals that ties humans together in great endeavour, and creates meaning and significance in life. Many could argue that increasing shareholder value or raising more funds is the overarching goal for a business or charity, and of course this is true. But if raising funds or increasing shareholder value are outcome goals (lags), the focus goals need to be directed towards what you are doing (lead) to achieve these results.

If 'amplifier' becomes the job description written in invisible ink on your business card, the training begins right now and continues until you stop—living that is. The tools and techniques explored in the following pages are all progressive: you can take first steps in each category of tool. They are all designed to help you with your intent to influence and inspire the people around you towards compelling, better futures.

CHAPTER 6

Speakership: the missing link

Public speaking is the first and primary tool of amplifiers; it's not really optional, but it requires little in the way of investment, other than time and effort. You can amplify one to one, but it's better to be able to leverage one to many and deliver your ideas and messages in the form of a public address. Speakership is leadership. It is the missing link between strategy and execution and is the simplest, most effective tool available to the leader who amplifies. Done right, it's a powerful tool that can, over time, turn things around.

This chapter explores the different dimensions of the speaking role and sets out eight different ways you can deploy speakership through a culture. So—game on—motivational leaders: you now have to become motivational speakers. Woo! I can feel your excitement.

Here is the thing: it's not as bad as you think.

A little rah-rah goes a long way, as long as you stay focused on results and keep the eight roles of the public speaker in mind, continually shifting through them so that you don't become a clichéd, metaphor-using, over-the-top vocal electric jolt.

Now put yourselves in my shoes for a minute: formally trained in scientific method at the University of New South Wales with some super proud parents—right? Instead of pursuing further academic success or even working in some scientific technical capacity, I became an aerobics instructor.

Anyone who has had anything to do with the fitness industry understands amplification. To wake up at 5 am on a Sunday morning and elect to move 150 people through some gruelling activities, despite the fact that they are hung-over and dealing with the results of a tough working week, requires a brave soul. But that's what you have to do, and you learn really fast what actually works; you learn how to get inside tired minds and weary bodies and find hidden resources.

My career moved on into adult education and corporate training, and eventually motivational speaking, but I never forgot the lessons I learned around energy and motivation in the fitness industry. They stand me in good stead.

At gatherings, my father would always proudly introduce my three older brothers: number one—a local entrepreneur done-good and turned-politician; number two—an engineer who basically makes massive projects finish on time and on budget; and number three—a classically trained musician and super-practical dude who can hot wire an ignition or rewire a house in a snap. And then there is me—the motivational speaker.

It's as if the parents of motivational speakers need to be reminded that they have children who have chosen that as a career. It's barely acceptable to call yourself a motivational speaker in Australia, and I totally get it. It has taken me years to not only be okay identifying myself as such, but also to be able to proudly claim that it's what I do, and furthermore, suggest that everyone should get on board the motivational leadership wagon.

This cultural cringe—my family experience—is exactly why this book is needed now. The need for motivation, inspiration and transformation—the need for amplifiers—has always existed. What we need now is an upgrade: essentially 'you can do it' just doesn't cut it, and I'm not sure it ever did.

Many who have the job title of CEO are also motivational speakers. I have met leaders of local government councils who are motivational speakers. I have seen principals of schools deliver addresses to the weekly assembly that are truly motivational. No matter what your job is or whatever it says on your business card: if you are an amplifier you have a job to do; sometimes you are a motivational speaker.

Before I launch into the eight roles of speakership and how they play out, it's worth scoping the game at a high level.

The battle for hearts and minds

When you step up as a motivational speaker it pays to know what game you are playing. Amplifiers understand that there is a battle to be won, but it's not on the field: the battle lies within the hearts and minds of your audiences. Your audiences may be staff, peers, your boss, your competition, your customers—anyone you need to persuade to follow you.

If the heart is symbolic of the emotional and creative side of people, let's make the head symbolic of the logical. There is an additional dimension, though, that needs to be factored in: we need to also consider that when you speak, you are sometimes informing people and sometimes inspiring people. Getting the mix right between these two axes is critical to hitting the mark as a motivational speaker and leader (see figure 6.1, overleaf).

As you can see in figure 6.1, inspiring the left brain is all about painting a picture of the future. Inspiring the right brain is all about bringing your ideas to life and giving them energy. You can see that informing the left brain is all about joining the dots and reaching informed conclusions, while informing the right brain is all about sharing the way and giving people a methodology.

Figure 6.1: the four roles of a speaker

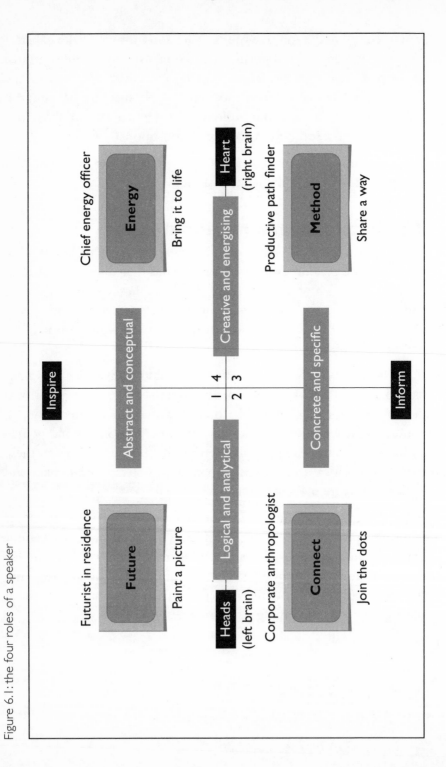

The four departments of motivational speaking

Great motivational speakers undertake eight functions, which may be fitted into four roles of work. Much like a business has sales, service and distribution departments, a speaker has four key departments that serve several functions. The heads of each department are futurist in residence, chief energy officer, corporate anthropologist and productive pathfinder. Sometimes, as a professional speaker, I'm expected to play only one of these roles. More often than not, though, it's my job to play all four roles, and to blend them seamlessly. Most amplifiers will find themselves doing the same.

The four roles and their main activities are:

- The futurist in residence captures the attention of the room.

- The chief energy officer makes it all look possible.

- The corporate anthropologist can make sense and meaning of all that is happening.

- The productive pathfinder scouts for strengths and weaknesses and keeps us on a critical path.

The first role of the amplified speaker is to show what is next. In my head, when I am in this department, I say to myself, 'Paint a picture'. It's about the actions we will take and about bridging the gap between the present and the future. You can tell when a speaker is in this department because they take examples from other industries that may apply to the current one. They discuss trends and make predictions. Often they will show the predictions as patterns, not specific events (this being a path that is always safer and easier to take). The two skills you need in this department are those of pattern recognition and prescription—the ability to move from data to conclusions and on to action. It's about 'Get up and do it!'

The second role of a speaker is to substantiate the claims in their speech. In my head, when I am in this department, I say to myself, 'Join the dots'. It's about logic and reason, and explaining why what you are saying is true. You can tell when a speaker is either in this stage of a speech, or playing this part at an event: they will use data and statistics heavily and will build a logical argument where known truth 1 leads to suggestion 2, which then flows into theory 3 and is backed up by example 4, and so naturally comes to conclusion 5 with recommendation 6, all of which are neatly lined up and backed up with convincing, real-world evidence. The primary skill you need to work in this department is the ability to make a convincing case. It's about 'This is why it is the right thing to do!'

The third role of a speaker is to make the agenda seem possible. In my head, when I am working in this department, I say to myself 'Show the way'. It's about skills and capabilities, either developing them or reminding people that they have them. Often you can tell when a speaker is in this department by the way they encourage sharing, relationships and collaboration. This is very much a 'we' department. You may be using case studies and examples from organisations or industries that are already leading the way, which others can use as models. The primary skill you need in this department is the ability to instill confidence and certainty. It's about 'We can do it together!'

The fourth role of the amplifier who speaks is to capture the attention of the room and engage the audience. Fire the room up. The last speaker at a conference is meant to do this, and motivational speakers generally sit in this last role. In my head, when I am in this role, I say to myself, 'It is time to bring this to life'. It's about using my energy to shift the energy in the room so that people are ready for the next stage. The primary skill you need in this role is the ability to grab the audience and get the attention focused. It's about, 'Let's do it!'

Let's see how you might work with these different departments in real-life speaking situations.

Over the course of a one-day program there may be four primary speaking slots of 90 minutes in length (though I know that would be a long time for most of us).

Session 1:	9.00–10.30 am	This is the 'paint a picture' role.
Break		
Session 2:	11.00 am–12.30 pm	This is the 'join the dots' role.
Break		
Session 3:	1.30–3.00 pm	This is the 'show the way' role.
Break		
Session 4:	3.30–5.00 pm	This is the 'bring it to life' role.

Session 1 is all about compelling futures. The job of the first speaker is to mobilise us in pursuit of a better future. The session 1 slots can be taken by anyone, but this speaker should typically be someone who is going to be present on the execution of the plan that has been outlined—someone who can say 'we' are doing this and 'I' am doing it with you. It's a 'lead by example' kind of role.

Most of the second session slots are death by PowerPoint—sleep-inducing data dumps. Using the ideas in this section of this book, you should be able to play the role successfully by keeping the engagement levels in the room high. It's the right time and place for the data; it's just typically poor execution that makes us question putting the CFO on early in the program. If they were more anthropological, helping us understand the meaning behind the data or evidence they are showing, then these sessions would come to life.

Most of the third session slots are given to the general favourite—the head of HR or a popular member of the executive team who has strong person-to-person rapport and who is highly believable. It is their job to build trust around the message, and to build the confidence in the room. They often show their support to the leader who spoke first, and by doing so, they also lend a common touch to the direction and agenda for the day.

Most of the fourth session slots are given to the people with the highest profile and greatest clout. In the past, where positioning and title immediately engendered respect, this was a legitimate strategy, but that's not really true today. If the person with the most titles also has the ability to fire the audience up, and can harness the techniques of evangelism and modern motivational speakers, then go for it (but, by the way, most don't). To play all four roles in a single speech is mostly about following the order, in, say, a 60-minute speech:

First 15 minutes — Show what is possible (paint a picture).

Next 15 minutes — Substantiate the claim (join the dots).

Third 15 minutes — Make it look possible (show the way).

Last 15 minutes — Capture the attention of the room (bring it to life).

You don't need to lock yourself into this agenda as a way of delivering presentations, but it is a useful order of events. Amplifiers know how to play each role, either by design or default. Knowing that you know these departments, you can fast-track your way to awesome presentations.

Sitting across these four departments is a set of eight specific roles.

The eight roles of speakership

The model shown in figure 6.2 illustrates how the eight functions and four departments all relate to each other. You will see how some, such as future builders, overlap two departments. In the case of future builders, you are simultaneously painting a picture and bringing things to life. The north, south, east and west points on this model are dual department roles. These four are the primary amplifier roles. The other four are dedicated to the department they reside in and so become secondary roles most of the time.

The four primary functions

The four primary functions are:

- future builder (the north)
- language codifier (the south)
- storyteller (the east)
- navigation expert (west).

Figure 6.2: the eight functions of a speaker

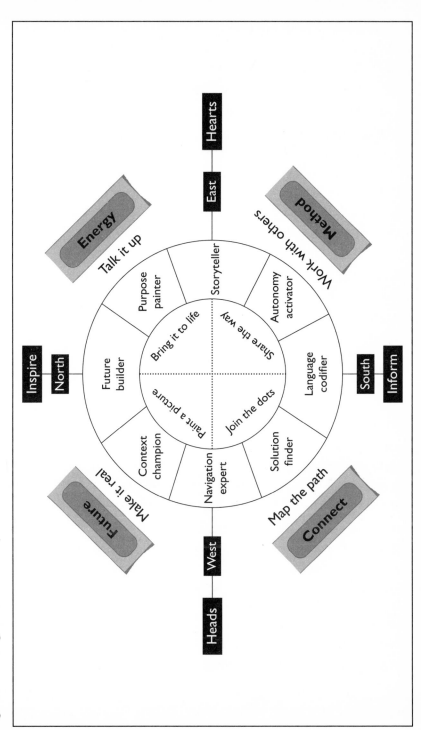

Future builder (the north)

Amplifiers are in essence *future builders*, able to compel a group of people towards a better future. This role really is the true north on the amplifier's compass. Everything makes sense through this future focus. If nothing changes, then what's the point of amplifiers?

So what amplifiers need to do is bring into today a future that is already in existence somewhere else. Futurist Craig Rispin, author of *How to Think Like a Futurist*, calls it 'redistributing the future'. A dentist may look to what's happening in retail optometry to see a commercial solution for their own industry or business. An engineering company may look at a graphic design business to incorporate the future of engineering as form and function — engineering as art maybe?

Nils Vesk, an innovation guru and author of *Ideas with Legs*, says that the most successful innovations out of any patent office on the planet are usually not the single wild, crazy idea that worked, but rather the combination of two or more patents combined in some way.

Being a future builder is not about predicting the next great thing so much as it is about creating it.

Language codifier (the south)

Amplifiers are masters of the word. They can turn a phrase to suit a situation. They are well read and they establish language and identify the language that becomes code for culture. Words have power. The most powerful words become the lexicon of a community.

Mantras, such as Barack Obama's 'Yes we can' campaign, are a perfect example of this. Being a language codifier is about not only understanding the jargon of a group but also continually refreshing its meaning. An amplifier can create many versions of their key ideas. They create them with a variety of linguistic palettes: formal and casual, technical and lay-person; as questions, as statements; and many other variations on this theme. The idea is to choose the right language to suit the situation and audience.

Quite often being a language codifier is not about creating new language or new meanings: it's about expressing complex ideas in a simple manner and saying things again in such a way that people get to hear them again as if for the first time.

By codifying the language a group uses and by understanding the power of words, amplifiers can ground people to established meaning. Everyone gets on the same page. Codifying language is very powerful!

Storyteller (the east)

Another primary role amplifiers work on is the role of *storyteller*. Amplifiers unpack the implicit success stories in the business or group. You don't have to be a great storyteller to do this first step: simply get people to share stories. Use customer or team panels, and this way others will share their stories, elevate role models within the business and simply interview them about 'How they do what they do'. In this way you start to activate the process of amplification, even if you are not a great storyteller.

The next step is to become a better storyteller. Joseph Campbell's *The Hero with a Thousand Faces* is the seminal work on the subject of storytelling. This book has sparked a movement of people dedicated to what has become known as the Hero's Journey, a series of sequences and steps that explore the perfect story structure.

The Hero's Journey gets quite convoluted but in essence this is the process.

1 Starts off bad somehow.

2 The hero gets a message to change.

3 They resist.

4 They accept the shift and step into it.

5 Relationships are formed.

6 They are tested by someone or something.

7 They get something magical.

8 They come out on top.

9 They get the glory.

There are many different resources for developing your storytelling skills, but the key thing to understand is that stories work. They get into peoples' heads and are one of the most powerful ways to communicate messages.

Navigation expert (the west)

Amplifiers are obsessed with results. They understand that false promises and un-met expectations are crippling to the culture of high performance, expectations and hope. Amplifiers are able to identify the next few steps in the path and, as a result, they can help a group navigate their way through and change.

The amplifier does not have to have all the answers: their skill is in knowing the questions to ask. A smart strategy for amplifiers is to continually focus the team on a question. The question may be 'What question needs answering here?' or it may be 'What decision do we need to make here?' Focusing on the next steps and progress keeps a group moving, and a body in motion stays in motion. Amplifiers keep the corporate body moving, progressing and taking positive next steps.

The four subsidiary roles

The other four roles, or points on the speaker's compass, represent a level of detail we probably don't need at this stage, but here is a quick overview of them. You can read more about these on the *Amplifiers* website. Simply go to www.amplifiersthebook.com and click on the 'speakership' link. These roles are:

- purpose painter
- autonomy activator
- solution finder
- context champion.

Purpose painter

Helping people understand the higher sense of purpose around what gets done by the group is a leader's role. Amplifiers direct the group's attention to the first, second and third horizon strategies in a 'forward into the future' way. At the same time, they remind us why we are doing what we are doing. This is done at a functional level, a community level and a level of intention.

At Thought Leaders, for example, we have a curriculum focus, helping clever people to be commercially smart; and a community focus, so we can be inspired by the company we keep. Our intention is to elevate consciousness. The amplifiers in our community remind us of these and give us a sense of purpose no matter how mechanical our game inevitably becomes.

Autonomy activator

Dr Elise Sullivan, a medical emergency expert, says in her doctorate thesis that there is a collaboration/autonomy paradox at play in most groups. She contends that for people to work brilliantly together they need to understand that they must not disappear as individuals. Contrary to the military adage that 'There is no "I" in the word team', she contends the exact opposite. High-performing teams are full of self-actualised individuals.

Autonomy is essentially the freedom to go about doing what I do without strict oversight or micromanaging. It's said that a person's degree of happiness is directly proportional to their degree of control. This freedom, of course, needs to earned. The circle versus triangle discussion explains this balance (see p. 53).

Solution finder

Because amplifiers have a bias towards action and results, they need to be solutions focused. Give amplifiers lemons, and they will make lemonade. They are resourceful and strategic around such questions as 'What problems need discussing?' 'What decisions need making?' and 'What actions need taking?'

Amplifiers look outside the world in which they operate to try to discover new solutions that they can apply to their people, their organisations or their personal challenges. They are continuously scanning the environment around them. They look at new social trends, new technology trends, new economic trends, new environmental trends and political shifts in order to bring this knowledge back to the tribe.

Context champion

The final role of the amplifier is one of holding the space for the big ideas and concepts that drive the group. This is often described as strategy or context or the meta that sits over matter. Whatever you call it, it's about the themes at play and about maintaining perspective on these regardless of the drama that's playing out in the business.

Dr Wendy Elford wrote her PhD thesis on the future of work and explored the theme of why work is not working for many. In her opinion, the skill of pattern recognition is the critical key to building work environments that allow people to work.

Context champions maintain a view of the big picture themes and act as masters of perspective, essentially seeing not only the forest, but also the trees. They understand that the map is not the territory but use context and the big picture to keep the group on track.

Attention up

When you speak, you need to pay attention, but not just to what is going on inside or even around you. The key difference between those who are good on stage and those who are truly world class is that best speakers pay attention to different things, or more accurately, to additional things. They still know what's going on inside and around them, but they have lifted their attention to a higher place. There are six things you pay attention to as a speaker. You can focus negatively on yourself (not very helpful), exclusively on the audience (equally unnerving) or start to focus on the four constructive levels of speaking. Speaking gets better when you build conversations with your audience, have something solid to say and stay aware of the different techniques and methods great speakers use. Nail these and you achieve the final stage: you can turn up authentically as yourself, amplifying those parts of you that help get the message across. Figure 6.3 shows the six levels of attention as rings.

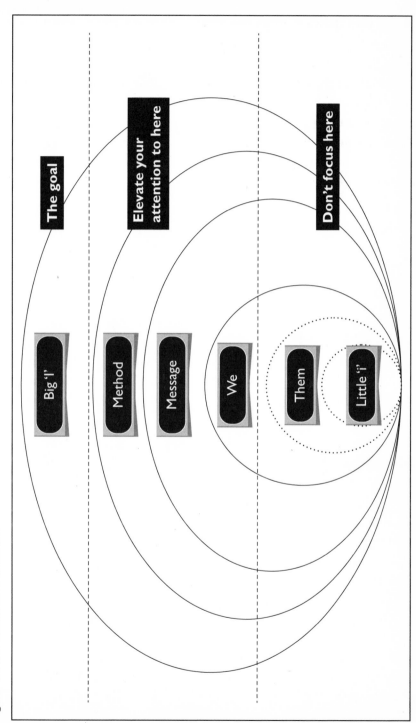

Figure 6.3: the evolution of attention

Ring 1: little 'i'

If you focus on 'you' when you speak, you are bound to be undone. In your head everything becomes an 'I' issue. 'I' am not prepared; 'I' am not qualified; 'I' am not wearing clothes that make me comfortable. These concerns are not some kind of narcissism, but rather the natural result of speaking in front of so many people. First step: you need to get over yourself. In this ring, you should quickly coach yourself and replace the negative self-focus with the question of 'What can you offer that may be of service to the room?'

Ring 2: them

Most of the advice you get on how to handle nerves comes from this centre of attention. Well-meant advice, such as 'Picture your audience naked' and 'Stare at their foreheads', is simply not helpful. It's a distraction strategy used when treating people with phobias. That's an acceptable strategy if you are planning to speak once in your life for 15 minutes, but it's not okay if you are committed to being a world-class presenter. To become rock-star good, you need a more successful coping strategy than simply 'getting out alive'. The next few rings (see figure 6.3) get you out of the survival mindset and get you thriving as a speaker.

Ring 3: we

This is the first of the elevating rings. The three elevating outer rings of conversation, message and method all work together to help you truly manage your internal state and keep an appropriate level of focus without becoming overwhelmed by the experience. The conversation ring is about getting into a dialogue with your audience. It may mean opening with questions—in a smaller audience, for example, by asking them what they already know or think about your topic. With larger audiences, you may send out a survey in advance to poll their opinions and to ask them what their biggest challenge is regarding your area of expertise. Increase the use of rhetorical questions with very large audiences: this creates a more conversational style.

Ring 4: message

You have to have something to say that is worth listening to. That seems obvious, right? It's amazing, though, that with the survival mindset, we are okay saying something that is obvious, already understood and easily read or reviewed outside of the live experience. When preparing a message for a live audience, you need to spend more time on the words, the key ideas, and the ways in which you can use repetitive variety—saying things more than once because they aren't listening—to bring the thoughts out of your mind and pass it to theirs.

Ring 5: method

Start to think about how you say what you are saying. Develop a third-eye perspective through which you begin to watch the science and art of oration. With this external view, you will begin to have an out of body experience when you speak. You become detached from the words and start to look at the way you are engaging with the room. It becomes a Zen-like experience as you metaphorically float above yourself while you speak, and you have an expanded consciousness/awareness of all that is going on around you. You notice small things, like that guy in the third row who picked his nose, the CEO nodding in agreement to your message, the CFO on her phone emailing someone in accounts to hold off on paying the catering bill. The trick is to stay engaged and connected with what is happening in the room and to have a range of techniques you can use to change the direction, energy and feeling in the room if you see it drifting away.

When you are controlling your internal dialogue—aware of the needs of your audience, engaged in the conversation with the room and delivering a message that they value in a way that is compelling—there is simply no time to get nervous. So, start from the outer rings and work back through rings five, four and three—and then two and one will take care of themselves.

In a way, this whole book is organised around helping you get to the outer rings when you are presenting. So every idea is a conversational 'we' idea, a 'message' construction idea, a 'method' delivery idea or some combination of the three.

Ring 6: big 'I'

When you step through these first five rings you get to the end game, you are amplified. You become yourself, but with volume. Not a loud, self-important noisemaking self. But rather an elegantly very present self. An idea we could call Amplified authenticity.

In the end, it all comes down to knowing with certainty that this 'public speaking thing' is something that you want to do, replacing negative, destructive thought patterns with such great productivity that there is no space in your mind for that kind of self-indulgent, downward-spiralling nervous tension.

Presenter evolution

As you watch different presenters and listen to what they say and how they say it, you may notice some distinct differences. A sports person who has just won the gold medal in their event may be sharing the story of how they did it. A consultant on customer service may be sharing steps to improve your service for customers. A spiritual guide may simply sit in service, involved in what appears to be an off-the-cuff, yet profound, question and answer session. They are each setting a state of energy in the room.

What follows here are my thoughts on the evolution of speakers (see table 6.1). It lays out an easy-to-follow process for taking your presentations to the next level. Once again, it's not how we normally see things: each stage is '*and* also', not 'then *next*'. It's about incorporating the best of the early stage stuff in table 6.1 into each next progressive level. This is the key to getting better exponentially at speaking, by building your next understanding on the foundations of your previous knowledge. I think mastering your attention through the levels in table 6.1 is the determining factor between competence and mastery.

Table 6.1: speaker stages of growth

		Stage 1	Stage 2	Stage 3
1	Focus	I	You	We
2	Process	Stories	Steps	States
3	Form	Theatre	Show and tell	Conversation
4	Evolution	I have this	You do this	Be this
5	Outcome	Stimulate	Impact	Transform

First stage

Kids at primary school operate in the first stage. A 5-year-old will present a message from his point of view (I) and will deliver his message through narrative (story). Assuming you are interested in the child and his stories, which of course the parents are, it's compelling. For motivational speakers, this stage is used to stimulate interest and is often best delivered with a semi-theatrical style: 'An amazing thing happened to me the other day…'.

Second stage

Teachers tend to work from this stage most of the time. They will set out a sequential process (steps) and deliver it with a training outcome approach (focused on you). The idea is that you acquire a new skill or a way of doing something. This stage is designed to impact the audience in some way, and is very much delivered with an instructive show and tell style: 'Here is something you may find useful…'.

Third stage

A great coach with an elite sports team will often present in this third stage. They use tone, and shift the energy in a room. Their message is all about the energy or mood (state) they create. Often they challenge, confront, excite or inspire, depending on the outcome they are hoping to facilitate. The third stage is very much about getting into the heads of the audience members and connecting with them in some significant way (engagement). This is the stage from which most change occurs: 'Together we can create history here today, but you have to want it badly enough. Do you want it? I know one thing: Physical pain disappears but the feeling of defeat lasts a lifetime ...'.

CHAPTER 7

Tongue fu! Noise versus signal

There is no doubt that we are living in a noisy time. It seems that lots of people want to be heard and they are shouting for attention. Great amplifiers are able to separate the signal from the noise. They do this by thinking, communicating and leading all the time. This is the three-step formula for amplifiers. Chapter 8 looks at the thinking part of the equation, and the whole book explores the leading part. This chapter and the next will continue to widen the conversation around the communicating part of the formula.

Communication is measured less by what you say and more by what is heard. Talk as much as you like, but if the message is not getting through then you are not communicating. Too often leaders say 'message delivered', without checking or doing anything they can to ensure 'message received'.

Communicating is the main leadership activity of amplifiers. But while speakership is the first and primary tool of amplifiers, it is only one of six communication channels available to them. In this chapter we will explore the other options. Speakership rah-rah is the first among equals, but dedicated amplifiers will want more modes of influence than simply speaking in public.

Amplifiers need to be world-class communicators. They need to be black belts in tongue fu—the martial art of the amplifiers. Instead of kicking, throwing and punching, amplifiers are telling, showing and asking. Amplifiers require both flexibility and capability in equal doses. They need to develop a broad capability to communicate in the various required situations, and they also need to be able to shift how they are communicating as required.

Six modes of communication

The six modes of communication are:

- speaker

- author

- trainer

- mentor

- facilitator

- coach.

'Tell' moments are where you deliver great ideas through stories and examples (content). 'Show' moments are where you deliver messages by sharing ideas and principles (concepts). 'Ask' moments are where you use the power of questioning to lead people through your messages. Sometimes you do this directly to individuals one on one and sometimes to groups. Amplifiers know how to use these various channels to communicate effectively.

We suggest you package your leadership messages so that they can be delivered across all or any of these six skills (see figure 7.1). The trick to this is to unpack your messages at three levels. This three-tiered thinking strategy is explained in more detail in chapter 8. At a high level you want to make sure every idea has a big picture theme, a clear point and a relevant example to back it up. These then become three distinct—yet aligned—components: a content piece, a concept piece and a context piece. You use all three elements when you communicate, but one of these three takes priority depending on the channel or mode you are presenting through.

Figure 7.1: tell, show, ask and the six modes of communication

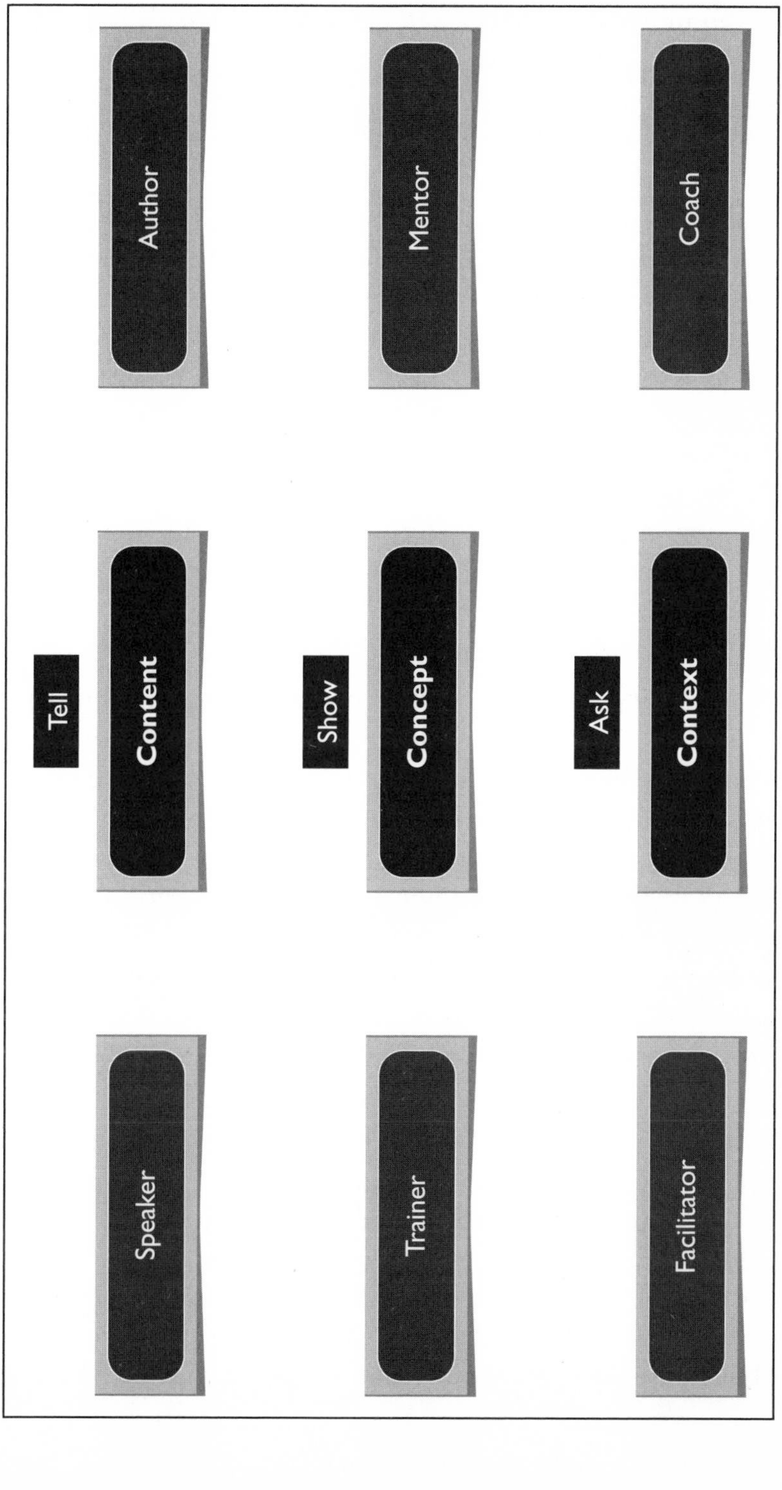

Tell	Content	Speaker	Author
Show	Concept	Trainer	Mentor
Ask	Context	Facilitator	Coach

The **tell** modes are mainly about content.

The **show** modes are mainly about concept.

The **ask** modes are mainly about context.

Speaker

The first mode of communication is speaking. When you are presenting at conferences (*speaking*) be sure to focus on *content*. For example, tell stories that inspire or use relevant case studies to link what you say with the audience's world. You may unpack a three-step process, share some facts or reveal some very telling statistics. The job of the speaker is to help a whole group of people to get onto the same page. The trick here is to have one big idea that acts like an organising filter for all your stories, examples and prescriptions. You bring your message to life!

Trainer

When running a workshop with a small group of people (*training*), be sure to focus on the *concept*. Your job in this mode of delivery is to show all you can about an idea. This is more about revealing information in a staged manner—showing step-by-step what's involved in the idea you are sharing. At this level the sharing of information needs to become interactive. The interaction is not random though—it is precise and focused on the specific point you are making. A useful formula or process is the *you*, *they*, *we* approach: first introduce an idea by *you* talking for a bit about it, then *they* talk to each other for a bit about it and then *we* all talk about the key idea in a group discussion.

Facilitator

Leading conversational discussions (*facilitation*) is a key empowerment skill of amplifiers. Essentially it's about skilfully setting up an environment in which people feel comfortable enough to share their ideas and opinions on a particular matter. These sessions can become 'talk fests' where all that happens is that people vent random thoughts and the outspoken people are the only ones who get heard. The trick is to use intelligent questioning to elicit thoughts and opinions around a central context. Great facilitators balance the opinion of the room, ask questions and keep the conversation going by allowing people to express their stuff but not letting the conversation become *about* the stuff.

So, in group environments, amplifiers can speak, train and facilitate their way around any key ideas that need to be shared. But amplifiers don't only communicate in group environments. Awesome amplifiers also work directly with key people to influence and share messages. A key role of amplifiers is to create other amplifiers. This is often best done, at least initially, in a direct one-to-one channel.

Author

Writing a message (*authoring*) and sending it, either in a fast way such as email or a considered way such as a strategy report, is a key capability of amplifiers. Amplifiers use not only the synchronous skill of verbal communication, they also create message ripples that continue long after they stop communicating. They draw ideas on coasters and napkins; they build slide decks that summarise a key idea; they send memos and craft reports that quite literally keep everyone on the same page. Amplifiers are often the authors of the strategy — the ones who participated in the thinking that directs our efforts.

Mentor

A critical idea in any group is the sharing of wisdom (*mentoring*) — passing down ideas to the next generation. Some professions have this in a formal process, such as apprenticeships or partner–associate structures. Regardless of whether this process is formal or not, amplifiers need to use their experience to build future capability in their teams. If we accept that amplifiers enlist others to also act as amplifiers, then this mode of communication is the trick to making that happen. Cultures that create and leverage amplifiers take the sharing of wisdom very seriously and formalise the process if at all possible.

Coach

Finally, the sixth communication mode is the conversational process (*coaching*) of helping people discover their own answers to the questions and challenges they face on a daily basis. Coaching is a powerful skill for amplifiers as it helps maximise the knowledge and confidence of the people being coached. It builds resilience and confidence so that the various members of the team are able to tackle problems independently.

Applying the six modes of communication

Leaders are expected to communicate effectively in a range of situations (see figure 7.2). The masterful motivational leader in the business context has six primary focuses:

- strategic authoring (authorship)
- leadership speaking (speakership)
- expertise mentoring (mentorship)
- training capability (expertise)
- coach confidence (empowerment)
- facilitate solutions (engagement).

Figure 7.2: six modes of communication and the big business questions

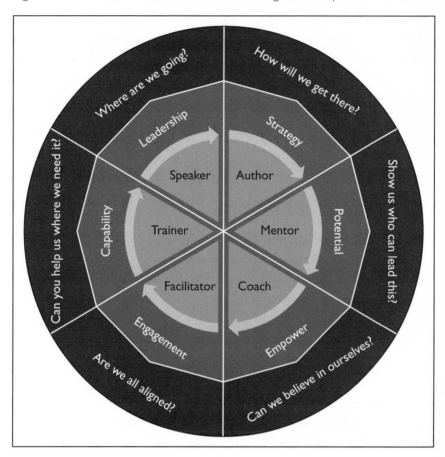

Strategic authoring (authorship)

Your first job as an amplifier is to understand and create a plan for achieving the organisation's goals. This first dimension is hardly ever a solo pursuit, but it is the responsibility of the senior leader to author, craft and design a compelling plan for achieving some desired future. This first skill answers the question 'Where are we going?'

Leadership speaking (speakership)

It's important that leaders share their vision for the organisation with others. To do this well they need to be able to communicate ideas simply and in a way that inspires others, regardless of the complexity involved in the organisation's path. This is about weaving stories and examples of the milestones and next steps required to move forward to progress the organisation's goals. It is essentially answering the question 'How will we get there?'

Expertise mentoring (mentorship)

If leadership is about bringing out the greatness in others then mentoring is the conduit for that function. Mentoring is essentially about knowledge sharing—it's about utilising experience. To do this well, the knowledge in key people is captured, packaged and delivered to others. Mentoring is about answering the question 'Who will lead us in the future?'

Training capability (expertise)

It is not the leader's role to develop capability in others, but it is their responsibility. Essentially leaders need people around them who are capable of making well-informed decisions. This often requires embracing new knowledge or effectively upgrading existing knowledge. The leader needs to know the gaps and get help to plug them. Learning and development is a leadership tool—too often it's delegated at both a strategic and an operational level. A leader should, by all means, have others work out a plan, but the reasons for the plan and its direction are not up to others. It is a form of resourcing and it answers the request 'Can you help us where we need it?'

Coach confidence (empowerment)

You can't be everywhere and you can't do everything. This simple idea is what lies beneath the leadership coaching function. Coaching is about empowering others; it's about replacing fear with confidence; and it's about enabling a group to solve problems in a future that has not been experienced yet—solving problems with no precedents. Coaching as an idea answers the often unasked but implicit question 'Can you help us believe it's possible?'

Facilitate solutions (engagement)

Driving a sense of ownership and the desire to work with initiative and autonomy is critical to organisational growth. The best-laid plan will go awry if people don't feel that they understand it and their role in it. Facilitation is about creating alignment between departments and divisions. It's also about creating an environment in which people see how their desires, goals and values match those of the group and their colleagues, and the organisation as a whole. Without this a leader's ambitions are unsustainable and are unlikely to be realised in a fast changing world.

Six capabilities for the modes of communication

Amplifiers need to consider six key capabilities for each of the six modes: that's one major and five minor skills that you will need to develop. This is a beginning and there is plenty more you can learn over time. Right now though let's just focus on what gets you up and running. Mastery is a great pursuit, but often one achieved at some commercial cost. Speak well enough to share your ideas, coach well enough to serve your ideas, but leave mastery for later. In other words, get on with it—then when you are up and running, get good at it.

When to use which mode

Remember in a business or organisational setting you will need to select the most appropriate channel for the outcome that you desire. Be careful not to get 'stuck' by using just one delivery mode to get your message across. Everyone knows a Senior Leader who only has the ability to tell people what to do in large meetings, then retreats to their corner office waiting to see the results.

These skills take time and many amplifiers effortlessly demonstrate them naturally. Your task is to select the right channel for the right person at the right time!

CHAPTER 8

Memes: the essence of an idea

Motivational leaders use the structure of ideas to make a difference: they really do need to think before they speak. An idea that is well constructed becomes a meme—it is able to be shared in a lot of different ways to people of all levels of understanding and still maintain its structural integrity.

The word 'meme' originated with evolutionary biologist Richard Dawkins's 1976 book *The Selfish Gene*. Dawkins wrote that evolution depended not on the particular chemical basis of genetics, but only on the existence of a self-replicating unit of transmission, and in the case of biological evolution that is the gene. For Dawkins, the meme exemplified another self-replicating unit with potential significance in explaining human behaviour and cultural evolution. The term meme has become synonymous with ideas, particularly ideas worth spreading.

Malcolm Gladwell, business journalist and author, wrote in *The Tipping Point*, 'A meme is an idea that behaves like a virus—that moves through a population, taking hold in each person it infects'. Ideas that move through society are built on what is often referred to as social object theory. Put simply, what idea have you heard today that would make it to a dinner party tonight? Motivational leaders take the time to study the architecture of ideas and use this to increase understanding and the influential impact of what they are communicating.

It's clear that ideas exist. They are, however, intangible, which creates a problem when leaders are communicating their ideas. A chair has obvious form, but an idea does not. Ideas exist in the space in-between. They exist in the space in-between your ears, the space that hangs between what I say and what you hear, and the space that exists between a problem and a solution. Physical objects have dimensions that make them real, such as width, height and breadth. Memes also have dimensions that make them real if you use them. Let's call them the north, south, east and west dimensions (see figure 8.1).

Full spectrum ideas

The key to creating great messages is to structure them so that they dance across the full spectrum of left brain logic through to right brain creativity, and then from concrete specific examples up to high order contextual ideas.

As expressed in the spectrum model in figure 8.1, you can see that every idea exists at various levels of abstraction (the vertical axis). At one end of the scale, you have very concrete expressions of an idea; at the other end, very abstract expressions of it. Tracking ideas across their compass points (speaking metaphorically) is an important part of motivational leadership.

Ideas also exist at various levels of logic and creativity (the horizontal axis). Just as we need both hemispheres of the brain, we need to mix logic (logos) and emotion (pathos). We need to have our ideas available so they appeal to both logos and pathos.

When you try to connect with someone, the attempt can be seen as a battle between putting in too much information (the south point on the model), resulting in the essence of the idea being lost, or making the message so simple (the north point on the model) that it is not seen as practical or relevant by those listening to it.

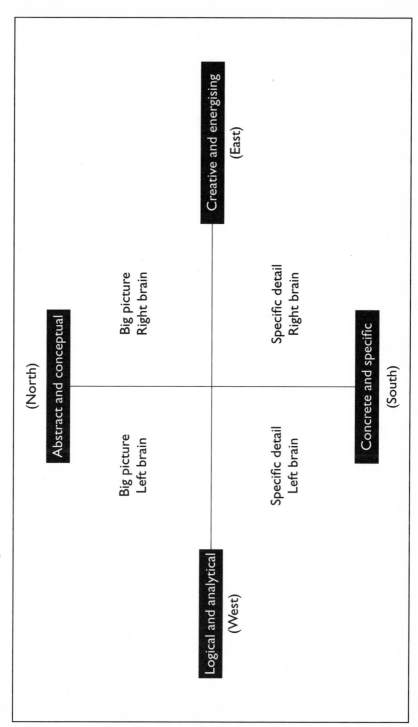

Figure 8.1: full spectrum thinking

The motivational leader creates full spectrum ideas. They know how and when to develop and deploy any or all of the five components of an idea (see table 8.1).

Table 8.1: the five components of an idea and their application

Refer to figure 8.2	Component	Example	Application
1 Context	Left brain context	Model	Gain consensus
2 Context	Right brain context	Metaphor	Embed understanding
3 Concept	Key point or meaning	Key point	Cut to the chase
4 Content	Logical evidence	Case study	Back it up
5 Content	Emotional engagement	Story	Make it memorable

Unlocking your expertise: intellectual property snapshots

The five components of an idea are also mapped out in the intellectual property (IP) snapshots set out in figure 8.2. Each idea expressed on one of the sheets is a meme: 'an idea that behaves like a virus'. The five components are:

1   model

2   metaphor

3   key point

4   case study

5   story.

There is a certain architectural element to thinking before you speak, and this structure or design helps you engage more people more of the time. It's about seeing an idea in all its layers simultaneously.

For ease of understanding, let's limit the layers of an idea to three: the stuff you say that is specific (content); the point you are making (concept); and the big picture theme that that idea is a part of (context).

Figure 8.2: the five components of an IP snapshot

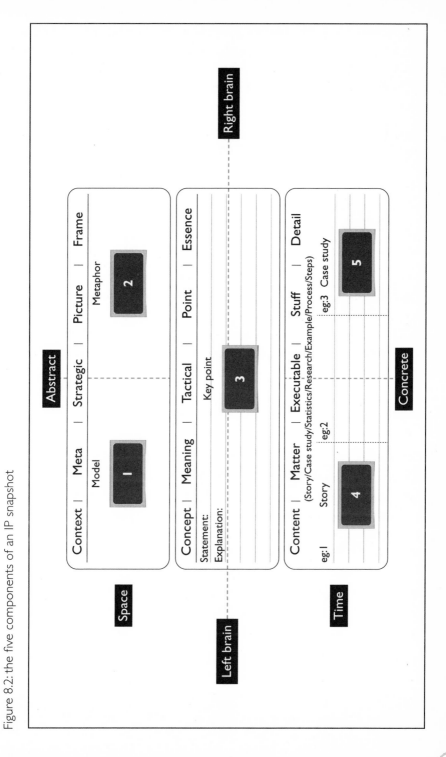

The stuff you say must make a point that ties into, and paints a picture in, the minds of others. So: stuff, point, picture. It is important to remember these three simple things around every message. Initially, you will need to craft a set of points (concepts) and then find different ways of expressing them (palette) so that you can communicate your message in a memorable way. Next, build a big picture (context) for the points. The big picture needs to embrace both the logical (left brain) and the creative (right brain). Finally, you need some supporting information (content) for your ideas.

Within the thought leader community, the intellectual property snapshot, often referred to as a pink sheet (because it is printed on pink paper) is seen as central to being able to craft a compelling message.

Each idea or main point you want to make should be represented on a single snapshot. Using the snapshot format creates a depth around your ideas and forces you to create messages with substance and balance. Figure 8.2 shows there are three clear sections to a snapshot. The first is the *context* section at the top; the second is the *concept* section or middle third; and the last is the *content* section, at the bottom. A snapshot mixes these three together to communicate ideas with structural integrity so that what you thought as a leader and what gets heard match up.

The context takes up space in people's minds, and the content takes time to share. The figure eight overlay on the snapshot represents this. Your key idea or point of concept should take very little time to communicate and by its nature take up very little mental real estate or head space in the minds of your audience. Throughout the explanation of the theory in this chapter I will run a practical example at each step around the idea of 'the evolution of selling'; this idea will work as a concrete walk-through of the principles.

Creating context

One way to create context—the idea's context—is to develop a visual model of your ideas. Creating context above every point you want to make is a master thought leader's tool. Context is the 'big picture' representation of your idea. Often this is a diagram, a model, a metaphor, an allegory or some applicable quotations.

Context provides a broad framework to give people a map to a message or line of thought. People are often engaged as they understand the purpose of the detail, and if they get lost, they can refer to your initial map.

To create context, the first row in figure 8.2 (p. 115), you can use models (marked 1) and metaphors (marked 2). For the example I have chose expanding circles for the model as they imply growth and the metaphor of evolution is embedded in the ideas itself. So the top of the IP snapshot would look like figure 8.3 (overleaf).

Models

Models are at location 1 in figure 8.2. A model is geometric in nature and consists of squares, lines, circles, triangles, pentagons, graphs and every variation and combination of them. At its simplest expression, a model is a visual representation of your key ideas using squares, triangles and circles. There are four main types of ideas you would communicate in the form of models. These correlate closely to Bernice McCarthy's 4MAT model of 1986. They are why, what, how and if. In figure 8.4 (see p. 119) they are expressed as a set, with some example models placed alongside.

Whether a model takes the form of a quadrant, some concentric circles, a pyramid or even a simple triangle, it helps you make more than one point. It helps define the conversational boundaries of any discussion.

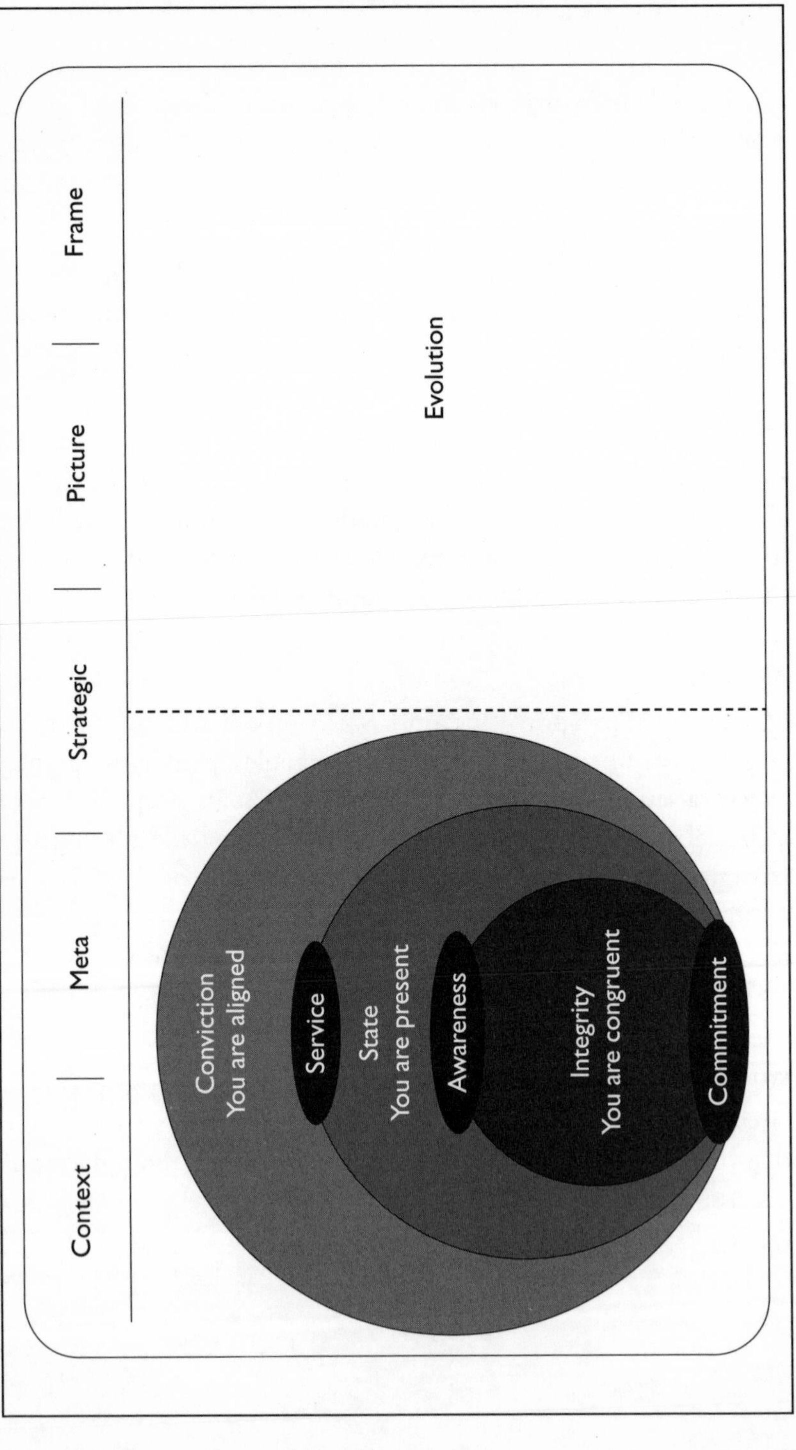

Figure 8.3: example of the context layer of an IP snapshot

| Context | Meta | Strategic | Picture | Frame |

Conviction
You are aligned

Service

State
You are present

Awareness

Integrity
You are congruent

Commitment

Evolution

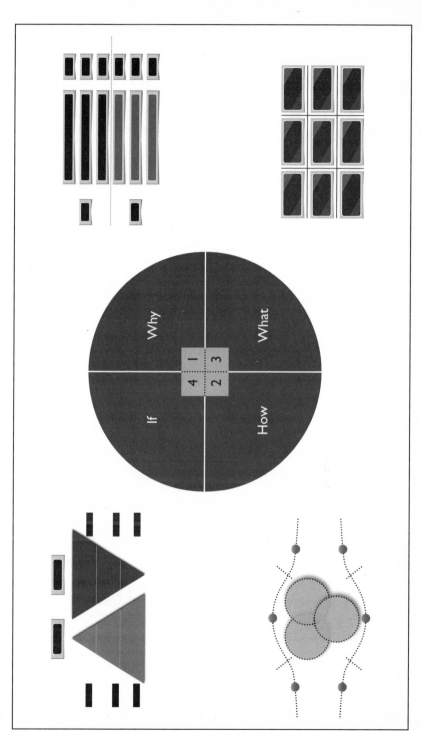

Figure 8.4: why to if process with model thumbnails

Some classic models you may be familiar with include:

- Maslow's hierarchy of needs

- Dr Stephen Covey's first things first model

- Robert Kiyosaki's cash flow quadrant model.

Become a model kleptomaniac. Capture and clipboard on your computer every model you see so you can study the anatomy of models, tracking their structure, design and intent so that you can more confidently develop your own.

Use the combined power of models and metaphors to capture your idea to affect both the left and right hemispheres of other people's brains. Models are a fundamental tool for a thinking motivational leader. They enable you to capture ideas with elegant simplicity. It's for this reason that they are first among equals when it comes to the five components of a meme.

Here are five thoughts to help you when working with models:

- *Your geometry teacher lied to you!* When creating models there are only really three basic shapes: a circle, a square and a triangle. Build your models from these.

- *Layer your models.* Each model should be able to be revealed at three levels of depth: the first is the awareness, the second is the distinctions and the third is the prescriptions.

- *Snapshots multiply fast.* One great model may make several points and so will be duplicated on a bunch of snapshots such as the one in figure 8.2 (see p. 115).

- *Work the intersections.* On every model you can often create finer distinctions if you work the boundary lines on the shapes.

- *Mix it up.* Balance your geometry, try not to have too much of the same model in all your IP.

Creating metaphors

Metaphors are at location 2 in figure 8.2 (see p. 115). Metaphors are object and activity-based, and can be sourced from real life and everyday examples. Some examples include instruments, household objects, hobbies, sports and environments.

Here are five thoughts to help you when working with metaphors:

- *Metaphors are personal.* The best metaphor is not always the one that fits your point perfectly but rather one to which you can bring some enthusiasm and know-how. A metaphor is a chance to show more of you and bring a multifaceted persona to your ideas and communication.

- *Clichés don't just happen!* If you are going to use a cliché metaphor, own it and explore the metaphor to its nth degree.

- *A question of detail.* A metaphor and a story can have the same structure and vibe—the metaphor is often the story minus the detail.

- *Stick figures must die.* Don't draw a metaphor. A metaphor is by definition a word picture—don't draw it unless you have wicked illustration skills.

- *Don't suck up.* The best metaphor is one that brings a different experience into the room. It's better to pick a metaphor you understand completely than one that you think may fit your audience.

Models and metaphors are not the only tools of context, but they are a great start.

Creating concept

If the context is the big picture themes around an idea, the concept is where you give those themes specific meaning. Love is a theme; unrequited love is a concept. Your concepts are the point around which your models, metaphors, case studies and stories pivot. In the example of the evolution of selling my concept may be expressed as shown in figure 8.5 (overleaf).

Figure 8.5: the concept or point as an example

Concept		Meaning		Tactical		Point		Essence

Statement: *All grown up*

Explanation: *Gone are the days of transactional selling. The power of the buyer and their product knowledge before*

they meet with you have changed the selling dynamic for the better. It's now a mature process of 'tell me

what you stand for and I will decide whether I want to buy from you'.

The key idea

Be clear on the point of your idea—why are you talking about it to this audience, or what difference will it make to this organisation, for instance. We call this the concept—it sits in the middle of the snapshot at location 3 in figure 8.2 (see p. 115) and is shown as a worked-up example in figure 8.5. You should be able to summarise your idea in one or two simple sentences that explain the whole point of what you want to communicate. From this singular idea, you then can create several different ways of delivering it. The point becomes the key identifier between one idea and the next. A snapshot may share a model (position 1) with another idea, but the IP snapshots don't share a point.

A tool for keeping thinking about your point on track is the idea of a consistent or deliberate linguistic palette. When coaching leaders around word choice, we map out their key ideas and then ask them to express the idea again and again in different ways. They may express the idea simply so that a 7-year-old may understand it; then express it inspirationally so that a 17-year-old gets into it; and so that a 37-year-old (practical expression) and a 70-year-old (sagacious expression) may understand it. This locking in and widening your different ways of making a point can actually help you think through and clarify what it is, exactly, that you are trying to say.

Here are five thoughts to help you when working with your key points:

- *Try the AB solution.* Each point you make should have a short, sharp, declarative statement (A), then a second sentence that explains your statement (B).

- *Book titles rock.* When making your point it sometimes helps to think of A as the title of the book and B as the subtitle.

- *Make your A sharp.* It's all about getting attention and cutting through the noise and information deluge.

- *Make your B clear.* The B in your point needs to be very clear and will often involve two or more ideas in relationship.

- *Make a PowerPoint slide of your As.* The declarative statement is perfect for your slide shows when accompanying a conceptual picture.

Creating content

To create content, the third row in figure 8.2 (see p. 115), you can use case studies (marked 4 in the figure) and stories (marked 5 in the figure). Gather examples, facts, stories and other detail elements to support or explain your point. We call this content. Like the big idea, you need to balance this to cover the whole brain. It's the stuff that people connect with.

In figure 8.6 you can see some examples. It's difficult and unnecessary to write out the content long hand on the IP snapshot. All you need to do is put enough detail in a bullet point to remember your case study or story.

Case studies

Case studies are logical stories. They are laced with facts and figures and should have a 'real life' feeling to them. You want to think of them as factual storytelling. They have a structure that flows from incident (what happened), to point (what you can conclude from the incident) and benefit (how you can use the information shared).

Here are five thoughts to help you when working with case studies:

- *Relevance rocks.* Make your case studies audience specific if you can. The best case studies are those that have huge amounts of personal relevance.

- *Be a scene setter.* Set the scene before you start the case study; explain why this case study matters and how it's illustrative of your point.

- *Stack statistics.* In the telling of a case study you want to have a few minutes where you stack a set of statistics on top of each other.

- *Introduce the complication or challenge at the start of the case study.* This is often best done as a decision the leaders had to make or a realisation that they came to which forced the change or key idea behind the case study.

- *Show pictures.* Show pictures of real people and real places as you unpack the case study.

Figure 8.6: the content as an example

Content	Matter	Executable	Stuff	Detail
	(Story/Case study/Statistics/Research/Example/Process/Steps)			
Example 1	Example 2		Example 3	
Cisco conference speaker strategy	Infographic on B2B sales		My story of buying the	
as case study	and marketing preferences.		Lexus — long version	

Stories

Here are five thoughts to help you when working with stories:

- *It's not all about you.* The easiest story to tell is one about someone you admire.

- *Silly me.* If you tell stories about yourself, do so in a self-deprecating way.

- *Follow the formula.* Joseph Campbell created a story arc format of the Hero's Journey (see chapter 6). Follow it when you create your stories.

- *You, now and then.* Stories are great when they are a mix of personal, topical and historical.

- *Stories are drama.* So act them out; become characters; use accents; and bring the story to life. Relive the story—don't recount it.

General stuff

Present your ideas left to right. When you are presenting an idea to a sceptical audience (or really most audiences), it is smart to present the logic case first (model, element 1) and case study (element 4) and the emotional case second (stories, element 5) and metaphors (element 2).

Time and space! Content takes time to get through. Context is quick but fills up the space in someone's mind.

Don't stuff up. Ideas are better created from context down—content (stuff) is time consuming and often audience-specific.

The content matters to your audience, and relevance is achieved through content—re-use is achieved through concept and context.

Prepare once—use often. The snapshot process is a leverage tool. It lets you take one piece of thinking and repurpose it into many different situations.

Read like a thought leader. Readers read about a great idea and say, 'What a great idea'; teachers ask, 'How can I share that?' Thought leaders ask, 'What do I think about that?'

Yes *but*, yes *and*. Great ideas are often built from the contribution to an existing idea or the contradiction of it.

CHAPTER 9

Tuning in to leadership

My mother is a great pianist and always has been. Her pet hate is a piano that is out of tune—to her it's an abuse of power. She knows that music when played well can move mountains and change the feeling in a room dramatically. To this day she travels to retirement homes and with a merry bunch of singers lightens the mood of the residents. She is an amplifier.

This lifelong love of piano means that as a child I got to watch tuners adjust pianos in church halls, our home and wherever Mum might play. She simply won't play on a piano out of tune. Watching these master tradesmen open a bag full of tuning forks, each set to a different frequency was something wistfully magical. They would tap away repeatedly on a particular fork until the offending string was tightened (or occasionally loosened) until the correct note was achieved.

Amplifiers do this with culture: they tune in and tune up a community by hitting a set of notes. These notes then set the tone for culture and set it on a course for excellence. Amplifiers have at least nine different notes they can combine. These nine notes ring across the three platforms of leadership, culture and work.

The nine notes you can play

In the nine-notes model in figure 9.1 (overleaf) you can see the rows are organised across these three focus goals: work is the foundation; culture is the glue; and leaders are the force that drives it all forward.

Figure 9.1: the nine notes of leadership

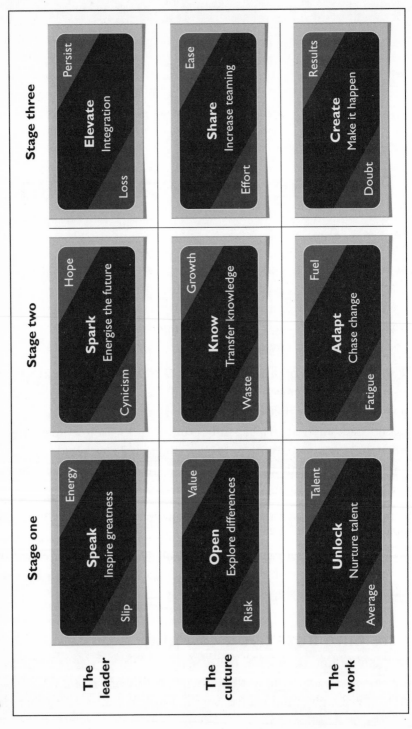

The nine notes have also been organised vertically into staged columns. Trying to focus on all nine notes at the beginning of a business, culture and performance turnaround will be overwhelming and unproductive—a cacophony if you like. Focus first on only one note in each focus goal at a time. Each additional stage is then iterative and inclusive of the previous results.

Unlock: work stage one

For this whole idea of amplification to work, you have to buy the idea that average is not acceptable. Many people have gone further than they thought they could because someone else thought they could. The work for the motivational leader is initially about identifying and developing talent in and around you. Know what your own strengths are, and your weaknesses too. Look for areas of expertise and talent, and begin to recruit and enrol your people into work groups of complementary talents. This builds a respect that helps drive the first cultural note you need to tap.

Many organisational development initiatives over the past 50 years have been driven by a focus on people fitting in and having a set of useful capabilities. For instance, if an executive is not very good at listening, we send them to active listening classes; if they are a little too task-focused, we send them on courses that will help them improve their emotional intelligence. The main tool organisations have used in the development of these well-rounded executives is the 360-degree feedback tool—essentially a survey that is conducted up, down and around you about what you are good at and what you need to improve upon. These ideas then inform a personal development plan designed to help the individual become a more well-rounded, contributing member of the team.

This is a very management-based approach. We can couch the feedback in terms such as 'constructive' and 'useful', but for many the experience is a bit like a partner who points out your faults and tells you that who you are is basically not good enough. Hardly inspiring, and in most cases resulting in a relationship breakup. Long-term relationships are based more on what we admire in the other person, not what we dislike. Focus on what you don't like and it's over; focus on what you do like and the relationship is more likely to work.

The alternative to focusing on the negative is focusing on what works. One method that is gaining traction in this area is called appreciative enquiry — looking at the qualities that an individual has that are special, and harnessing these strengths to achieve more. In their book *The Appreciative Inquiry Method*, Frank Stowell and Duane West, academics at a UK business school, have been credited with the development of the appreciative inquiry method (AI) and they explain it this way: 'Appreciative Inquiry ... starts with the belief that every organisation, and every person in that organisation, has positive aspects that can be built upon. It asks questions like "What's working well?", "What's good about what you are currently doing?"'

Some researchers believe that excessive focus on dysfunctions can actually cause them to become worse or fail to become better. By contrast, AI argues, when all members of an organisation are motivated to understand and value the most favourable features of its culture, it can make rapid improvements.

Fundamental to the idea of AI is a focus on strengths. The Gallup organisation has done some great work on this and their two graduate thought leaders, Marcus Buckingham and Tom Rath, have both written great books on it. In *Strengths Finder 2.0* Tom Rath explains the power of focusing on strengths and talents:

> People who use their strengths everyday are six times more likely to be engaged on the job. People are at their best when they are able to use their talents and abilities — the traits and behaviors at which they naturally excel. Empowering your people to discover and develop their strengths will position them to do what they do best every day.

Focus on talents and strengths of the individuals and you will be able to drive better collaboration. When we accept that we are imperfectly perfect, we can drive more effective team building. We can engage our people around what they are good at versus what anyone can do. Leaders need to look for the special and nurture the different and, as a result, tap into talent more effectively. This will allow you to attract, retain and develop the best and brightest. This is the first note you need to tune the organisation in to.

Five taps that ring the nurture talent note

- Become obsessed with talent identification, development and leverage.

- Understand how leading talented people differs from traditional management.

- Develop a focus on uniqueness and consider an appreciative inquiry approach over 360-degree feedback.

- Become strengths-centred and build teams around complementary strengths.

- Link talent to commercial advantage by exploiting expertise to grow business.

Open: culture stage one

Once talent has been nurtured you have the seeds of understanding based on respect. People begin to see that, to be extraordinary in one thing, they often need to see an extreme gap in another. This gap is often filled by someone who looks, sounds and works in a very different way from the first person. There is a great risk of conformity in a culture in which all people look, sound and think the same. Exploring differences is the essence of diversity. Once again, however, if diversity is the goal then a culture that is open and values differences is the focus.

When a culture is quite set in its ways it will struggle to survive. The first step in transforming a culture is for it to become more open. By opening things up, we move from the safe locked-down cultures that insulate themselves and huddle together away from the world of their customer or from emerging markets, to become explorers: exploring the power of different ideas, the challenge of thinking differently. It's hard to remain open if you are not secure in who you are and what you stand for. A fundamentalist, for example, is typically fearful: they are afraid that by considering a different way of seeing things they will be somehow polluted or tainted. This fragility is the core reason people stay closed and locked away in their beliefs and world views.

A diversity agenda is a good first step in this process, but simple transparency will also get the ball rolling. A culture that thinks it has all the answers is normally missing the key questions. History is riddled with examples of marketplaces, civilisations and businesses that failed to stay open to change and lacked the courage to step outside their convictions and learn something new. Transforming culture is about being open to the value of different people and ideas. The first step in building a culture worth belonging to is achieving openness.

Five taps that ring the openness note

- Explore ways to make the group more transparent.

- Start looking at ideas outside of the things the team feels comfortable with.

- Understand any race, gender or professional bias that may be closing down perspective.

- Formalise your diversity strategy.

- Set up free dialogue platforms, both physical and digital.

Speak: leader stage one

The leader's role in this first stage is to speak one to one and one to many as ways of encouraging people to be the best they can be. This creates an energy in the group that can be used to drive performance. Without a steady diet of communicated expectations, teams and groups can slip or drift back into normal ground hog days. The leader's role is to fight apathy and inertia, and to actually drive momentum.

If speakership is leadership then the missing link between a good idea (strategy) and people doing anything about it (execution) is the leaders ability the leader's ability to inspire people to want to reach the goal and to take the necessary actions to achieve it. If a leader does not get out among the stakeholders and start communicating with energy and passion there is a huge risk that the strategy slips into nothing. The strategy ends up being a bold statement with no energy behind it. The leader's work, their labour if you like, is to push against the inertia of the machine. The machine of 'sameness'; the machine of 'bureaucracy'. Status quo becomes the enemy when a leader seeks to transform a workplace and its culture. All great leaders find a way to inspire people with the vision. Speaking often and well is the first step to making this happen.

Speaking is about knowing when to tell, when to show and when to ask others in order to increase the engagement, the relevance and the meaning for every person enlisted to achieve the goals. You need to do this by exploring and answering the driving questions people have: what are we doing, how are we getting there and how long will it take? In later chapters I will drill down on some specific skills and techniques that leaders use to *speak* change into a business.

Five taps that ring the speak note

- Implement regular meetings.

- Undertake a 'meet the people' road show.

- Create and distribute message pieces prolifically.

- Mix the casual and formal opportunities to communicate.

- Train message champions to extend the reach.

Adapt: work stage two

Historian Arnold Toynbee famously said 'Nothing fails like success!' This mantra is the adapt or die imperative. Ask yourself a few basic questions. Is the world getting simpler or more complex? Are things staying the same or rapidly changing? Is it getting easier to compete or harder? Evolutionist Charles Darwin expressed it best when he said 'It is not the strongest or most intelligent of a species that will survive, it is those with the greatest ability to adapt'.

Easier said than done, right? Especially when everything that used to work is losing its traction. The move for leaders, salespeople and businesses to succeed in the future is to actually move from change *management* to change *making*. To shake up the status quo and choose the kind of future you want to be part of. Adaptation is less about responding to change and more about embracing it. Going into the eye of the storm and creating a better business or career from the middle of the turbulence is how you become future-proof—not standing outside like a helpless victim waiting for change to dictate your next course of action.

Constant innovation is the name of the game. Essentially what got you here may not get you there. Adaptation is about developing an appetite for change through growth. Not the indecisive change for change's sake, but rather building on what you have done as a strategic decision to become more agile and responsive to the environment around you. Change management as an idea has a kind of helpless nature to it. Change readiness has a kind of survival tone to it. Much better for amplifiers to be the change makers. This proactive approach to change then fuels performance without having an organisation's people ending up change fatigued, continuously complaining that nothing within the group stays the same for very long.

Five taps that ring the adaptation note

- Run regular scenario or hypothetical thinking workshops.

- Invite guest thinkers and speakers from seemingly unrelated industries into your space.

- Go on road trips and tour new markets.

- Focus on continuous improvement without keeping any attachment to what or how you do what you currently do.

- Kill your core business (hypothetically) and explore what's left.

Know: culture stage two

Once a culture is open and sharing, it starts to see the value in differences of opinion. The next piece of work culturally lies in breaking down the siloing of information in and around what you do. A culture worth belonging to has pooled, catalogued and made accessible the knowledge that is intrinsic and inherent. It takes this expertise and moves it from the implicit to the explicit, driving growth across the group and decreasing waste. Basically making knowledge accessible to all prevents reinventing the wheel and avoids the problems of history repeating itself.

This note is about working on breaking down knowledge hoarding, a concept that requires a shift in the power dynamics of a team or group. If knowledge is power (which I doubt is still true), then people tend to keep information close to their chest. It's a very bureaucratic quality and unfortunately it has run its useful course. The time is up on that organisational behaviour. *The New York Times* columnist Thomas L. Friedman wrote:

> We are shifting from a world where the key source of strategic advantage was in protecting and extracting value from a given set of knowledge stocks — the sum total of what we know at any point in time, which is now depreciating at an accelerating pace — into a world in which the focus of value creation is effective participation in knowledge flows.

Ideas are great, but only if we can do something with them. The increase in the accessibility of technical knowledge is staggering. The web made sure of that. So the new power is what you can do with information. The sheer physical impossibility of any one person or group hoping to explore all the applications of a piece of knowledge is obvious. You actually waste the information if you don't share it, so start giving your knowledge more freedom. Knowledge *applied* is power! Advantage is no longer in what you know, but rather in knowing how that knowledge can be utilised in the best way!

A culture or team that shares information effectively has a serious competitive advantage. Don't keep reinventing the wheel. Find ways to learn from the experience and lessons of others. Set up formal and informal information sharing across the group. Mentoring programs, communication cafés and family conferences are all examples of how you can formalise the transfer of knowledge. It's a waste to have knowledge and experience either not captured or under-utilised in a group.

Five taps that ring the note of knowledge

- Document what you know, capture it, package it to be delivered in and around your business.

- Be generous with expertise, as it forces you to apply the knowledge, not just hold onto it.

- Share more information across departments, divisions or any other divide.

- Cross-pollinate people and process to alter the cultural gene pool.

- Publish, publish, publish.

Spark: leader stage two

One of the challenges leaders face in their pursuit of transformation is the inherent cynicism that rears its ugly head in almost any group. My recommendation is that the leader takes a long hard look in the mirror, prepares for this in advance, and takes bold steps into the punch. Not blindly, but without any prevarication or hesitation.

The whole game of motivational leadership is hopeful! It is optimistic, and while it has room for questions, for thinking and for sceptics, it needs to have a zero tolerance for cynics. So start a spark, and make sure that, as a leader, you are catalysing hope and putting some energy into what your team does today to affect what results you get tomorrow.

The leader at stage 2 is trying very hard to start a rolling fire that wipes away the unproductive past and sets a new blaze in behaviours that will take the group, and everyone in it, to a better place. Leaders will find pockets of cynicism in the group as they begin to drive higher levels of amplification. Remembering that the three roles of a leader conclude with mobilising people in pursuit of a better future, it's essential that a leader find ways to make the future real now. This can be done by highlighting success stories, introducing case studies of success from outside of the group, and continually talking about the brighter tomorrow. This hope helps people to keep going when the results are slow.

Five notes that tune in the spark

- Focus on success stories and share them loudly and often.

- Learn from the past but don't live there.

- Create watershed moments where *what was* is recognised in ritual and put to pasture.

- Fan the flames. Find moments of success you can anchor the future to.

- Redistribute the future. Continually bring examples of where the future you are pursuing is being experienced already today.

Create: work stage three

High performers are less focused on the efficiencies of getting things done and more focused on what they are creating. High achievers know that when we are creating new and amazing things we lose ourselves in our work. This is not about being creative as an attribute or skill, but rather the lift we get when we feel like we have made something new, or put something into a form that it has not been in previously.

When work becomes creation we really begin to see results. It removes the doubt people have about what we are doing and where we are going. The things you create—your work results—are the milestones that link where you are to where you want to be.

Sparking up people's hopes will wear thin if you don't have a bias towards results and making things happen. Identify and showcase all results even if they are simply the result of learning why something did not work. This practical focus on learning and gathering evidence of wins is the key to making the whole motivational leadership game possible and sustainable. Motivational leadership really needs to be more than talk. Highlight success and gather evidence, no matter how small, of why the direction is right.

Five notes that ring the create note

- Launch pilots and run experiments.

- Make it real as quickly as you can, however you can.

- Identify discrete delivery milestones and celebrate and promote them.

- Break huge projects down into deliverable stages.

- Develop a version mindset, 1.0, 2.0, and so on.

Share: culture stage three

Once we have transferred knowledge or shared expertise within our group we need to push the sharing to new levels. A culture in which everyone has each other's back, versus one where everyone is *on* each other's back gets so much done through the generous nature of the people within it. Many hands most definitely make a lighter go of work. Like most stage 3 initiatives you can't jump-start this; it needs to develop within the group. It will take time, considerable effort and a huge generosity of spirit consistently and liberally applied at every opportunity.

The mathematics of sharing is very similar to the mathematics of compounding interest rates. The layered effect of 'sharing' over time creates an easing of the burden of productivity. In great cultures people often articulate how much easier it is to get things done than in other cultures they worked in. This is not the result of some singular initiative, but rather a function of the impact of a long-term consistent commitment to sharing the load.

In a culture that shares, teaming happens not by compliance or coercion but by natural attractions and fit. If you have great people, doing great work, they are attracted to play with others naturally. Organic teams form in corridors and work groups to help each other achieve amazing things. Teams' workflow is generally on show for all to see and contributions are not only appreciated but also actively sought.

The functional nature of sharing is around perspective. Physicist Albert Einstein said it so well: 'The significant problems we face cannot be solved at the same level of thinking we were at when we created them'. 'No one of us is as smart as all of us' is the mantra behind the concept of share.

Teamwork in a post-industrial world looks dramatically different from the way it did during the industrial period. The goal is still the same though. It's about decreasing effort and easing the journey. The classic sporting team analogies are instructive, but not a complete enough metaphor for most team environments. The key difference is to develop teams that are trying to do each other's work where possible, as opposed to trying to avoid work, or trying to take the glory. This outcompeting to share the load builds highly committed cultures of performance. No accountability performance review frameworks are required when this is achieved.

Five taps that increase sharing

- Eliminate the busy mindset.

- Get beyond mere 'deliverables' and incentivise 'contributables'.

- Invite different departments to comment on projects.

- Implement a fresh eyes program throughout your business.

- Invite people to explore random acts of generosity.

Elevate: leader stage three

There is a critical need for momentum in groups. Many ideas start with plenty of fire, and if results appear the team can often keep going for a while fuelled simply by their success. At some point, however, the group will need an upgrade. Progress is insatiable—the more you get, the more you want. A leader needs to recognise this and find ways to change the game. These changes are better if they are expansive, rather than simply distractive—not change for change's sake so much as change for impact's sake. It is totally about bigger games, better games and smarter games. Games that go from the finite and simple to the infinite and complex.

If you don't do this, the work will wither, the culture stumble and the performance drop. Basically, we lose our mojo. If you can artfully create new, exciting progressions in the game that helps us all achieve more, then you will be able to persist as a group and continue to perform with stellar results.

In old-fashioned analogue fantasy role-playing games there are players and what's known as dungeon masters (DMs). The DMs don't join in with the players: they are the directors of the experience. Their role is to keep the right level of challenges in the game and to ensure that players focus on the 'now', as only the DMs have the full story line.

Great leaders are scanning the next chapter, reviewing where we are in the playbook and communicating the now and the next. They help us be in the now while they keep an eye on the next. It's the leader's job to manage the delicate balance between success, results and the next stretch. The mojo that gets built up in the eight previous conversations is lost if new and exciting games are not created. This 'game fullness' approach to leadership is pure and is based on the science of drive. It's what has millions of gamers around the world investing hours and hours on play that simulates work. This may be the biggest idea in 21st century leadership.

Five acts that elevate the game
- Tell us what game we are playing.
- Build epic quests.
- Expand our limiting beliefs around what is possible.
- Talk in three levels: the stuff, the point and the big picture.
- Work with, identify and recruit courageous game changers.

Putting it all together
The work of a group is to unlock talent and use it to drive competitive advantage. At the same time the work needs to grow and evolve, continuously adapting to the pace of change in the world. The work needs to create. It's about making things happen, going from

talking about something to actually realising it. Seth Godin calls it 'Shipping—do something'.

The culture that supports successful amplification needs to be open to differences, recognising the value in difference and building robust frameworks for knowing when to agree and when to discuss, when to stand out and when to fit in. Again ask yourself 'Do we have each other's back, or are we on each other's back?' This culture needs to be generous with knowledge, continuously emptying the cup of wisdom into others. This drives growth and reduces the wasteful repeating of lessons already learned. Done well this should create a culture where workloads are shared. Instead of asking how can I offload this task, team members should instead be asking how can my doing this thing save my mate from having to do it. In doing so you are continuously freeing up talent to dive into the next big thing. Many assumptions around work ethic underpin this of course.

The leader then has the role of inspiring greatness in and around herself. By doing so she can keep the group's energy up and reduce the drift and slip that kills momentum. Cynics will arise as people give up but forget to shut up, but leaders need to keep energising people towards the future by instilling a realistic hope. People will then stay focused on the game dynamics at play that help all people do great work and maintain the drive to achieve.

You can download posters of the nine conversations as conversation starters from the *Amplifiers* website at www.amplifiersthebook.com. There is also a leader's guide that walks through how to have a conversation about the conversations. Reading back that last sentence felt a bit Zen, like 'how to start a conversation about conversations'; it's a bit like 'the sound of one hand clapping' or 'hold on tight with an open palm'.

CHAPTER 10

The 15 questions

I'm watching a master amplifier speak. She is polished in a way that suggests a presentation style earned by time on her feet. As the leader of her business unit, she is under pressure to deliver results, and a recent shift in business strategy is not helping. Status quo being the enemy of all new initiatives, she knows her message has to be heard and her team needs to embrace change. She also knows few people like change.

There are clues as to why one speaker is better than another, why one leader's words have more impact than another. One clue is in the focus of their message — is it 'I', is it 'you', or is it 'we' focused? Another clue lies in their awareness, innate or developed, around whether it's time to deliver the message, or whether the audience, the team, is not yet ready.

There are 15 questions listed in table 10.1 (overleaf) in the minds of your audience members that need to be answered before you can deliver the content of your message. These questions are often unconscious, but answering them in advance means that people are more receptive to what you have to say and more likely to remember what you have said. If the message you deliver is relevant, thorough, elegant and unique, then the audience just may act on it. The answers to these questions 'frame out' any concerns that may be present, position the amplifier with humility and enrol the senior or most experienced people in the room to your agenda. It's this process of framing that sets up amplifiers to succeed.

Table 10.1: the 15 questions

Priority	Positioning	Barriers	Switches	Action
x 3: Why you? **Credibility**	✓ 6: Why should I care? **Benefit**	✓ 9: What's wrong with the topic? **Message**	✓ 12: What's in it for me? **Intrapersonal**	✓ 15: So what should I do? **Prescription**
✓ 2: Why this message now? **Urgency**	x 5: What do you do? **Process**	x 8: What's wrong with them? **Audience**	✓ 11: What's it about? **Existential**	✓ 14: How is it unique? **Differentiation**
✓ 1: Why this message? **Importance**	x 4: Who are you? **Disclosure**	x 7: What's wrong with you? **Personal**	✓ 10: What's it like? **Abstract**	✓ 13: What's your point? **Clarity**
Lots on my mind!	**Who is this person?**	**Is this right for me?**	**What does this person even know about it?**	**You got me, what's your point?**

Making your message a priority

The first set of questions (numbers 1 to 3) is about making your message a priority for your audience. These questions take a busy person with lots on their mind and get them paying attention to your message.

1: Why this message?

The amount of information we could be exposed to is staggering. I read a piece recently that suggested that 3500 books are being written every day—a mind blowing thought—and the question is not, 'How will I find time to read them all?', but rather, 'Of those I choose to read, which ones are worth my attention?'

Sharing information in any other way is equally daunting: an audience gives you an hour of their time, so you had better give them something worth listening to. You have to get them to truly believe the main message of your presentation before they even begin to tell you what's on their minds.

To answer the question, 'Why this message?', you can do several things. Here are some ideas:

- Make the case for the message through case studies along the lines of, 'Here is someone just like you, who felt like you, and who took action A and has got desired result X'. You would then take the audience on a journey into the case study and show them how that person applied key ideas from your message to achieve a positive shift in their world.

- Link the message to some current positive or negative disruption event—game-changing events are always happening. They can be social, technological, economic, environmental or even political. You can hitch your message to this known and current event. While you explain the event, you are looking for metaphoric and literal nods of agreement in the room. Once you have achieved that, you can then present your key idea as an additional consideration or possible solution to managing that event.

- Link your message to some truism or adage—some universally accepted truth—that is generally accepted as a universal truth or immutable law; for instance, gravity, trust, that relationships take effort.

2: Why this message now?

One thing that is true for almost every audience you will address is the sense that they have a lot on, and that all of it is all-important. Stephen Covey's landmark book *The 7 Habits of Highly Effective People* attempted to address this issue and his following book, *First Things First*, precisely addressed the idea of conflicting priorities. I imagine this is an issue on almost everyone's mind in the developed world. This is something you need to navigate every time you are attempting to gather people's attention around your idea or cause. They must be inspired to give it a sense of urgency in their own work or lives!

To answer, 'Why this message now?', you can do several things. Here are some ideas.

Bubble head technique

Identify the primary issue on the audience's mind and link your message to that exact issue as the solution. You can do this by expressing a compassionate understanding of what it's like to live in their world—to be them. I visualise a bubble of inner dialogue floating above their heads filled with questions such as these: What do they say to themselves in the quiet moments at the end of the day? How would they express their biggest worry at the moment? I then overtly attach my speech and the key message as the solution to those questions.

Tease for attention

Create a vacuum with your language that teases attention. The end of each episode of your favourite TV program introduces some unanswered question that makes it a priority for you to tune in and keep watching the show (often at an inconvenient scheduled time). It's the cliffhanger technique used in writing fiction, so that each addictive chapter leads into the next, and you end up reading until 3 am, knowing that you should be getting to sleep. Marketers use this technique in direct marketing sales copy and there is some (small) benefit to elements of models in single-page direct marketing letters or websites. In essence, what you are trying to do is attach a cost benefit to the lack of—or giving of—attention to the message. For instance, you might say:

> In a minute, I want to share with you the moment I woke up to how critical this idea was to my career…

> The big idea I will share around [topic] will rock your world. I am in such a hurry to share it, but I know I need to slow things down and take you on the journey that got me to this place of true conviction around why this [key idea] is critical in your world.

> Just the other day, a member of my audience came up and shared with me how she had started to [topic] and what it had done for her life…

> If I had known this idea 20 years ago, I reckon I could have halved the time it took me to achieve X…

There is a fine line between teasing attention and simply withholding information in an annoying way, and you need to find a way to manage that.

Use urgent language

There are phrases and key words that we use when trying to convey a sense of urgency. Using these helps to answer, 'Why this message now?' Some example of words you may use to create this sense of urgency are imperative, immediate, imminent, looming, pressing, straight away, inbound, on the horizon, in the immediate future, within [specified time frame].

3: Why you?

This is where you begin to build credibility around both who you are and your message. I suggest you have a 'loose/tight' way of doing this. If you get a great response to your first two pieces around the message and the urgency of it, you can spend less time on the third credibility piece. If, however, you feel like you haven't been able to make your case, you may need to spend a little more time on the third question. Likewise, sometimes you are talking to an audience where most people know who you are, and so less on this third step is better; at other times, you may need to do a full length version of your answer to 'Why you?'

Positioning who you are and what you do

The second set of questions (numbers 4 to 6) is all about positioning who you are and what you do. Assuming you have the attention of your audience, you need to then establish your credibility with them. This is about letting them know a little about who you are, what you do and why it's relevant to them and their goals.

4: Who are you?

The critical thing whenever you talk about yourself as an amplifier is to do so humbly. Make sure you own your success, but be quick to share how you have learned from mistakes and failures. Bono once introduced his band through career analogies: The Edge was the CTO, Adam Clayton was CFO, Larry Mullen the Head of HR, then Bono introduced himself as the plumber—because he has to clean up the stuff that goes wrong. This self-effacing positioning is key to talking about yourself.

5: What do you do?

Think like an engineer as you talk through what it is you do and how you go about doing it. See if you can elevate others. State the fact that you are surrounded by some seriously smart technical cookies. You can say something like, 'I get all the credit but they do all the work'. Then proceed to explain how person X's genius allows you to get Y done better than others.

6: Why should I care?

Jump onto this sixth question as quickly as you can—you can skip over four and five if you are pressed for time but be sure to touch on this one if you can. To answer this question you need to link what you know to what people want. Explain how your X was designed to fix three known problems the audience would readily admit. If you can, link how what you propose helps the audience get what they are in business for (people get that you are delivering a message just for them) and addresses their real work challenges. This makes you super relevant.

Knocking down barriers and subconscious objections

The third set of questions (7 to 9) is all about knocking down barriers and subconscious objections. Be careful with the first two as they can be skewed by your insecurities in the first place and mass generalisations in the second.

7: What's wrong with you?

There is nothing wrong with you at all—I am sure 'to know you is to love you'. *But*, at some time in your life you will be the odd one—maybe you are short, maybe you are bald, maybe you are white and the audience is not. My friend and card-carrying amplifier WC Mitchell was horribly burned twice in his life—he is in a wheelchair and speaks about overcoming adversity. Seriously qualified right? When he rolls out onto the stage he immediately makes a joke in such a clever way about how he looks that you don't feel sorry for him and you immediately let go of the shock of seeing him for the first time.

Be careful that you don't come from insecurity when framing out a what's-wrong-with-you concern. Don't bring a problem into the room that doesn't exist.

8: What's wrong with them?

This is dangerous territory because if done in the wrong way it can lead to bigotry and assumptions that are flawed. There is kind of 'no return' from that place. You are going to have to learn from your mistake and go amplify somewhere else. The trick is to think through your audience and see if they have a professional bias or some such. Engineers over-specify things (such as bridges, so they don't fall down), accountants over-analyse things. This may get in the way of your message around minimum viable product and the need to launch faster to an engineering team, or taking more entrepreneurial risks to a team of accountants. That means their bias blocks your message. The trick is to frame the audience's bias in a complimentary way and position the disruption or change that is instructing your thinking. Ask for their thoughts, and then position your message.

9: What's wrong with the topic?

If a message is hard to swallow or you know something may be poorly received, it's useful to get that elephant out to the front of the room and name it. Often you can lay out past thinking, current thinking and future thinking in such a way that your message is the second or middle frame, and the current thinking is the old. By creating a third space bigger than your idea, you are showing that your idea represents a cautious evolution to new thinking rather than a revolutionary and binary conversation between your idea and theirs.

Switch the smart cookies on to your talk

The fourth set of questions (numbers 10 to 12) switch the smart cookies on to your talk. Howard Gardner (a learning specialist) identified three major learning or listening modes or switches that people choose when they are already reasonably familiar with your topic. These will need to be addressed even if your audience members simply think they know a lot about your topic. These three switches—the need to know your sources, the need to know what the big idea is and the need to know what the pay-off is—need to be turned off pretty early in your program. Fail to address these and about halfway through your download they may 'white ant' you, effectively undermining your platform.

10: What's it like?

This question addresses the need for referencing. Either literal references as in 'I read this book and it got me thinking', or some kind of reference to a past experience, such as 'Do you guys remember when Jonnie from accounts spoke at the 2012 conference?', or even using metaphors and analogies. Referencing helps people to see that you are not passing off other people's ideas as your own. Quote others, hold up books, make references or describe shared experiences, and use analogies to start your conversation.

11: What's it about?

This question positions your message into a primary overarching context. Basically, pick a word that sums up what you want to discuss and share it at the outset. Let's say my word was 'leverage'. I might start a one-on-one communication with 'Jenn, do you have some time to discuss a few leverage ideas I have?' Then, what you want to do is build a memorable phrase that anchors that word in a way that's easy to recall. In the example of the word leverage you might say 'I think we need to make the most of what we have'. This helps meta thinkers and people who are across the detail of what you are talking about find a way to engage with your angle. It's like a folder called 'leverage' opens up in their brain and all their knowledge and thinking filters through this, and they end up supporting your agenda.

12: What's in it for me?

The 'me' in this case may be 'my group' or 'my division' or 'my family', and it's not an unreasonable question for someone to ask. So many people are pushing their agendas that it's hard to separate the good from the bad. Take time to get really clear for your audience about what the pay-off is for them. Quite simply, stack at least three reasonable and realistic benefits, skills and positive outcomes that the audience can expect from your point, agenda or proposal.

Action and driving change

The last three questions (numbers 13 to 15) are about action and driving change. Amplifiers drive results and these three final questions are a result of all your hard work on the 12 previous questions.

13: What's your point?

By this time in the framing process we are ready to start delivering key ideas. Make sure that your point is clear and well articulated. Your three or so great points nest under your primary context (question 11). Make your point real. A good structure for delivering points is to think of them in two parts: the first being a short, sharp declarative statement, the second being a slightly more lengthy explanation. This is a direct link back to the idea shared in figure 8.5 (see p. 122). The goal is to lock in two sentences — one short, one long — that make your point.

14: How is it unique?

Make sure you can explain how your idea is unique — look for a point of difference. The easiest point of difference is to be a contrarian. Pick a sacred cow or an established thought and challenge it. A similar strategy is to target an enemy to your idea and place your key message in counterpoint to a well-established concept.

15: So what should I do?

Our final frame is the action frame. You need to have a plan of attack considered well in advance, otherwise it's incredibly frustrating — it's a tease and not much use. Once you have engaged people to a message and they are keen to understand your thinking, pick three, five or seven simple actions that people can take. Make them practical as well as conceptual.

The importance of sequence

Most people run the first three questions in reverse, and that is a big mistake. Here's why.

They start by establishing who they are; we have no reason other than politeness and respect to care, at this stage. Twenty or more years ago, people had respect for titles, positions and qualifications. Now, with so many transparent mistakes having been made by people and organisations with all three (Enron, BP and Bill Clinton, for instance) we have other expectations. Position and authority can no longer be used to garner our attention. This is the way we used to start speeches, but it just doesn't work with a sophisticated modern audience.

Then leaders have explained why we must listen to their message. This is always the second piece, so it's not misplaced; it just needs the frame of what you're talking about before it comes alive.

Only then do speakers give us a feeling of what they are going to say, which of course is much too late. The proliferation of readily available information on the web means an audience is conditioned to get to the point or an answer more rapidly. You can moan and say that we have lost patience as a society. I think we have simply become more discerning about who and what we pay attention to, and that's awesome if you have something to say that is valuable, and equally awesome in that it shoves the 'superficial' speakers out into the cold, where they belong.

The same three questions, answered in the correct order, create a completely different experience.

At a high level, it tracks like this:

I have a message to share and it is important.

Not only is it important, but I feel (and I am confident that you will as well) that it is urgent and that we should drop everything that is non-essential and focus on this now.

And in case you're wondering, this is who I am and why I have become the carrier of this message.

The Dale Carnegie program (still one of the best people leader programs on the planet, I reckon) is based on one of the all-time best selling books, *How to Win Friends and Influence People*. The program teaches young people the idea that no one cares how much you know until they know how much you care. This is true in the opening minutes of a speech. In one-on-one situations, the 'caring' Dale Carnegie is referring to is empathy, compassion and listening. In a group environment, such as a speech, it is about respecting who is in the room and showing some awareness as to what it is like to be 'them' for a day. So, by answering the three questions in sequential order, you get to do this.

You need to be clear on what is getting in the way of your attempts to influence and use the 15 key questions to frame these issues out and think before you lead.

Part IV

THE WHO

Amplification is as old as time. I am certain an early human stood on a rock in front of a cave and with a few 'uggs' and 'biffs' produced sounds to the effect of 'Let's go get that woolly mammoth and perhaps our kids won't starve this winter. Who's with me?' Motivational leadership is not only about group communication: it can be used just as effectively in one-on-one communication.

Okay, if you have got this far I need to make a bit of a confession: if you had not picked it up, I'm a bit into the heroic story — always have been. As I've aged I have come to realise that all heroes are flawed, and more interesting and complex than the goodies versus baddies game we played as children. But make no mistake, being an amplifier means walking the hero's journey. It's my fervent belief that this makes a difference and that the alternative choice is a sad one, a non-choice really. To believe that you can't make a difference, to live without hope, is to merely survive. I live by the idea that you are a difference maker, a thought leader, an influential player in this thing called the human race — in short you are an amplifier, if you choose that path.

In *Zen and the Art of Making a Living — A Practical Guide to Creative Career Design* (though the book is not only about career design) Laurence G. Boldt says:

> Heroic action cuts the bounds of fear and triumphantly asserts that there is a spirit in us that is noble and mighty. This loving spirit exists within all life, including yours. The heroic life lives in dormancy in all and in active expression in the great men and women.

Julien Smith touches on these themes in his extraordinary book *The Flinch*: what it takes to be great, to be heroic, with particular reference to 'world-changers'—those transformational individuals who make a difference—amplifiers! His book is in your face, borrowing from others and bootstrapping its way into your mind. A good read for the crazy ones.

This path has been trod before and the effect has been to create defining moments in history.

This section is about amplifiers in action, demonstrated through examples that are intended to inspire you as a leader. They form an anchor for those who choose to step up and lead in a way that transforms not only those around them but also the leader themselves.

CHAPTER 11

Amplifiers in action

Each example of an amplifier in this chapter highlights the two critical 'impact' stages on the leadership ladder: motivational leadership and inspirational leadership. Sharing the stories of these amplifiers is itself an act of amplification. If any of these stories encourage you to see the world anew and your role in it as one that influences others, my goal has been achieved. Many of the examples of amplifiers in action come from speeches. This is as much about the availability of those transcripts as it is about my obsession with public speaking.

Cicero's regret

This next story begins in the early evening on the steps of the Senate in Ancient Rome. It is the end of February 44 BCE, and a heavy speech session has just finished in the Senate. Gaius Julius Caesar, the most powerful man in Rome, had been voted in as dictator for life by the Senate. This granted him war powers that flew in the face of the idea of the republic of Rome.

Caesar's cousin Brutus, extremely jealous of Caesar's success, has lobbied covertly for the removal of his cousin through murder. It was planned for the Ides of March (the 15th of the month). This act, by the most 'legal' men in Rome, legitimises the murder as a quasi-judicial regicide (the execution of a king). It is this moment in democratic history that Shakespeare immortalised in his play *Julius Caesar*.

Caesar's intellectual sparring partner, Marcus Tullius Cicero, was unwilling to participate in the plan to assassinate Caesar. Cicero was Caesar's nemesis but he simply could not play a part in the violent act. But this famous bloody act is only a footnote in a superbly interesting time in the history of motivational leadership.

For centuries the leaders of the Republic of Rome wielded influence through the power of debate, public speaking and lobbying—motivational leadership at its best. A successful leader needed to engage with Roman citizens at all levels. Here are the five common levels explained.

- The common Roman citizen was appealed to with circuses and triumphs (grand displays and gifting). Caesar appeared and spoke at these public events and built brand Caesar as a result.

- The working-class man was appealed to through the people's assembly via outdoor meetings (mass crowd control).

- Soldiers were appealed to with hard-won truths (honest straight talk) shared on the eve of battle or the fields of victory, and often at the gates of Rome before the general led his army, without weapons or armour, at the end of the triumphal procession awarded to a general after a great victory.

- Influential families were appealed to through lobbying for favour (motivated self-interest).

- The best and brightest in the Senate were appealed to through logical argument and intelligent debate (laws, principles and arguments).

Caesar excelled at all five of these domains of influence. It was said that when Caesar spoke, men wept, but when Cicero spoke, armies marched. For me, Caesar represents all that is method-based in the art of amplification and Cicero everything that is message-based. Contemporary motivational leaders need to be a hybrid of the two styles.

If Hollywood were to cast the two in a movie today, Caesar would be played by Brad Pitt and Cicero, probably by Danny DeVito. Cicero was the antithesis of Caesar. Whereas Caesar had perfect breeding, looks and manly qualities, Cicero was not easy to like, was abrasive and did not carry the perfect family name. He was also a Stoic and as such rejected overt displays of emotion, didn't smile much and had some strong opinions on almost everything, perhaps the original inspiration for *Star Trek* Vulcans and Dr Spock?

Both Caesar and Cicero separately studied at the famous school of rhetoric in Rhodes run by Apollonius Molon. Here they learned the art of rhetoric: how to construct and deliver messages that would impact and influence others. This was unusual among most Romans but a critical part of their individual impact on Ancient Rome. Molon is famous for quoting Demosthenes (a fourth century Athenian orator) that the three most important elements in rhetoric were 'Delivery, delivery, delivery'. Demosthenes studied the best orators and inspired the methodology taught by Molon many years later to Romans. Bottom line: they studied how to become great speakers formally, because they knew it was the key to influence and power in Ancient Rome. It's not very different today—Speakership is Leadership.

Cicero, while not as famous as Julius Caesar (more thanks to Shakespeare than history), was way more prolific than almost any other Roman and was quite influential on Western writing, especially for the advancement of law as a profession. More of his speeches have survived than those of almost any other figure in Ancient Rome. These men seriously mattered to the organisation of the Roman Republic. Do you matter as much? Will you be quoted as much in 2000 years' time or even two years' time?

What can we learn from the Ancient Romans?

- Put in the effort to study communication skills. These guys spent time studying the art of public speaking.

- Adapt your message to your audience. Caesar, more than any others, had mastered the art of adjusting his message to suit different audiences in Rome.

- Leaders step up and influence en masse with public speaking. Speakership is an essential part of motivational leadership.

- The art of memorable phrasing is critical. Both Cicero and Caesar knew how to turn a phrase so it became a rallying cry.

- The battle between the two symbolic ends of the speaking spectrum—message and method—is over. Today's motivational leader needs both in equal doses. They need the message that matters, delivered in a way that inspires action.

Henry V

In the early morning of St Crispin's Day, 25 October 1415, King Henry V's English army, dysentery-ravaged and outnumbered, which had been marching for 17 days, found itself forced to give battle against the relatively fresh and numerically superior French army.

Shakespeare's classic play *Henry V* includes a famous speech in which King Henry speaks to the troops on the eve of battle. David McCubbin (Logie–award winning actor and Shakespearean superstar, graduate of Australia's National Institute of Dramatic Arts (NIDA), director, actor and corporate trainer) suggests that leaders practise giving this speech to get the rhythm and vocal modulation of a great Motivation speech.

> Once more unto the breach, dear friends, once more;
> Or close the wall up with our English dead.

Here we go—there is a lot at stake right now, I know you are tired but this is it, fire up.

> In peace there's nothing so becomes a man
> As modest stillness and humility:
> But when the blast of war blows in our ears,
> Then imitate the action of the tiger;
> Stiffen the sinews, summon up the blood,
> Disguise fair nature with hard-favour'd rage;

Hey, I know this goes against everything we have worked hard to achieve, but serious times call for a serious response. I also realise that most of the time we are pretty relaxed and chilled out. But I reckon we've got to get 'fired-up' about this one. So here is what you have to do.

> Then lend the eye a terrible aspect;
> Let pry through the portage of the head
> Like the brass cannon; let the brow o'erwhelm it
> As fearfully as doth a galled rock
> O'erhang and jutty his confounded base,
> Swill'd with the wild and wasteful ocean.
> Now set the teeth and stretch the nostril wide,
> Hold hard the breath and bend up every spirit
> To his full height.

See—that's how you do it—let's scare the daylights out of the competition!

> On, on, you noblest English.
> Whose blood is fet from fathers of war-proof!
> Fathers that, like so many Alexanders,
> Have in these parts from morn till even fought
> And sheathed their swords for lack of argument:
> Dishonour not your mothers; now attest
> That those whom you call'd fathers did beget you.
> Be copy now to men of grosser blood,
> And teach them how to war.

Come on, make your mum and dad proud. They worked pretty hard to give us this chance and I'm stuffed if we are going to let them down. Let's prove to those oldies that we can do just as good, if not better.

> And you, good yeoman,
> Whose limbs were made in England, show us here
> The mettle of your pasture; let us swear
> That you are worth your breeding; which I doubt not;
> For there is none of you so mean and base,
> That hath not noble lustre in your eyes.

Seriously, I know I'm a king and all that, but that's just my stuff. I reckon *you* are the kings, and just looking in your eyes I can see you are made of the right stuff.

> I see you stand like greyhounds in the slips,
> Straining upon the start. The game's afoot:
> Follow your spirit, and upon this charge
> Cry 'God for Harry, England, and Saint George!'

Well, enough of me gas-bagging. I can see you are good to go. It's game-on! So give it your best and give it one for your God, your country—good luck!

> Extract from William Shakespeare *Henry V*, Act III Scene I
> Commentary with apologies.

Stop now and perform those words, stand on a fake stage, tread the boards of your imagination and connect the words to your style. This is how we get amplifiers to become more dynamic in their delivery. Over-act this, then apply the tone to your relevant group communications. It's a great speech to try to embody the style of amplification.

Brother Bobby

Amid the tragedy of the assassination of Rev. Dr Martin Luther King, Jr on Thursday, 4 April 1968, an extraordinary moment in American political history occurred when Robert F. Kennedy, younger brother of slain President John F. Kennedy, broke the news of King's death to a large gathering of African Americans that evening in Indianapolis, Indiana.

The gathering was actually a planned campaign rally for Robert Kennedy in his bid for the 1968 Democratic nomination for president. Just after he arrived by plane at Indianapolis, Kennedy was told of King's death. Local police advised him not to make the campaign stop, which was in a part of the city considered to be a dangerous ghetto, but Kennedy insisted on going.

He arrived to find the people in an upbeat mood, anticipating the excitement of a Kennedy appearance. He climbed onto the platform and inquired as to whether or not the crowd knew that King had been killed, and then, realising they did not know, spoke off the cuff and from the heart. Here is what he said.

> Ladies and Gentlemen—I'm only going to talk to you just for a minute or so this evening. Because...

> I have some very sad news for all of you, and I think sad news for all of our fellow citizens, and people who love peace all over the world, and that is that Martin Luther King was shot and was killed tonight in Memphis, Tennessee.

Martin Luther King dedicated his life to love and to justice between fellow human beings. He died in the cause of that effort. In this difficult day, in this difficult time for the United States, it's perhaps well to ask what kind of a nation we are and what direction we want to move in.

For those of you who are black — considering the evidence evidently is that there were white people who were responsible — you can be filled with bitterness, and with hatred, and a desire for revenge.

We can move in that direction as a country, in greater polarization — black people amongst blacks, and white amongst whites, filled with hatred toward one another. Or we can make an effort, as Martin Luther King did, to understand and to comprehend, and replace that violence, that stain of bloodshed that has spread across our land, with an effort to understand [with] compassion and love.

For those of you who are black and are tempted to be filled with hatred and mistrust of the injustice of such an act, against all white people, I would only say that I can also feel in my own heart the same kind of feeling. I had a member of my family killed, but he was killed by a white man.

But we have to make an effort in the United States. We have to make an effort to understand, to get beyond, go beyond, these rather difficult times.

My favorite poet was Aeschylus. He once wrote: 'Even in our sleep, pain which cannot forget falls drop by drop upon the heart, until, in our own despair, against our will, comes wisdom through the awful grace of God.'

What we need in the United States is not division; what we need in the United States is not hatred; what we need in the United States is not violence and lawlessness, but is love and wisdom, and compassion toward one another, and a feeling of justice toward those who still suffer within our country, whether they be white or whether they be black.

So I ask you tonight to return home, to say a prayer for the family of Martin Luther King, yeah that's true, but more importantly to say a prayer for our own country, which all of us love — a prayer for understanding and that compassion of which I spoke. We can do well in this country. We will have difficult times. We've had difficult times in the past. And we will have difficult times in the future. It is not the end of violence; it is not the end of lawlessness; and it's not the end of disorder.

But the vast majority of white people and the vast majority of black people in this country want to live together, want to improve the quality of our life, and want justice for all human beings that abide in our land.

Let us dedicate ourselves to what the Greeks wrote so many years ago: to tame the savageness of man and make gentle the life of this world.

Let us dedicate ourselves to that, and say a prayer for our country and for our people. Thank you very much.

A powerful piece of 'speakership', this speech is carved on a bronze plaque as part of the *Landmark for Peace* memorial to both men in Indianapolis (even though King is buried in Atlanta), near where the speech was made, and in stone on Kennedy's own memorial in Arlington National Cemetery.

That night, because of Kennedy's ability to shift a crowd, to elevate their thinking, he was able to prevent violence, although riots were widespread in other cities on the news of King's assassination, and to start the healing and move a crowd of people from deathly thoughts and potential criminal acts. He moved a crowd to step into their best selves. He did it without cliché. He achieved it without ego. He simply stepped up and led. If that's not motivational leadership, I don't know what is. Robert Kennedy was a true amplifier.

Crazy Ones

Apple is often cited as a remarkable turnaround business and the late Steve Jobs as a remarkable turnaround leader. The Apple story, with its rise and fall and its position as a great disruptor, is now well documented.

Sam Biddle (Blogger), from Gizmodo (a trend and technology publisher), got his hands on an Apple genius team-training manual. Like a cold war operative, he sliced and diced it to understand what was going on inside the training of one of the most successful retail innovations of our age. Here, Sam comments on the training regime at work in the business of being Apple.

> Before you can don the blue shirt and go to work with the job title of 'Genius' every business day of your life, you have to complete a rigorously regimented, intricately scheduled training program. Over 14 days you will pass through programs like 'Using Diagnostic Services,' 'Component Isolation,' and 'The Power of Empathy.' If one of those things doesn't sound like the other, you're right—and welcome to the very core of Apple Genius training: a swirling alloy of technical skills and sentiments straight from a self-help seminar.

One of the greatest retailers on earth formally trains their shop assistants to use empathy, education and empowerment to sell more gadgets. They are not shop assistants or service repair technicians, they are 'geniuses'—and that in itself is genius. What would you rather go to work as, a computer repair technician or a genius? Who would you rather help you with your product and service difficulties, a technician who uses jargon to make you feel more stupid or an educator who makes you feel special?

You can go to the *Amplifiers* website at www.amplifiersthebook.com and click on the 'learning links' tab for links to the full article. Apple is teaching its geniuses to be motivational leaders, and doing so formally, deliberately and without any doubt that this method will, and has, impacted on the commercial bottom line.

This is not the first time that Apple has played with the word genius as a motivational idea. The way the culture at Apple uses heroic context to move people to action is remarkable.

A famous Apple advertising campaign ran in the 1980s around the message 'Think Different'. It celebrated genius and the individuals who made a difference and called them the 'Crazy Ones'. A cool video for the Apple fans on the *Amplifiers* website shows Steve Jobs discussing his vision for how the genius bar will work. Simply go to www.amplifiersthebook.com and click on 'videos'.

This ad and its various spin-offs became legendary as an example of turnaround and transformational marketing. It is also a great example of amplification. The focus is outwards—not inwards. Consider the tonal qualities for how they make you feel. Look at the key message for how Apple celebrates the difference that an individual can make and how talent trumps conformity. This is a key amplifier strategy: unlock talent, open up minds and inspire greatness.

The words 'think different' were created by Chiat/Day art director Craig Tanimoto. The text of the various versions of this commercial was written by Rob Siltanen and Ken Segall. Known as 'Crazy Ones', the ad was art directed by Chiat/Day's Jennifer Golub, who also shared the art director credit with Jessica Schulman and Yvonne Smith. It starts:

> Here's to the crazy ones. The misfits. The rebels. The troublemakers. The round pegs in the square holes.

At the time this ad aired, Apple CEO Steve Jobs was on his 'second-coming' at the company, having been ousted by the board years earlier. Here is what Steve Jobs said in an interview for the PBS *One Last Thing* documentary, in 1994.

> When you grow up you tend to get told the world is the way it is and your life is just to live your life inside the world. Try not to bash into the walls too much. Try to have a nice family life, have fun, save a little money. That's a very limited life. Life can be much broader once you discover one simple fact, and that is — everything around you that you call life, was made up by people that were no smarter than you. And you can change it, you can influence it.

I feel like I have to say 'Amen, brother Steve, RIP'. Apparently he was a tyrant in the workplace, but there is no doubt he was an amplifier. He did not suffer fools and expected his people to do work that was, in his words, 'insanely great'. Reading the biographies and public record accounts of his leadership style, it seems that he was a bit of a bully, but that unless you worked directly with Steve you would never know the truth of his leadership style. Without a doubt he had the 'expectation of greatness' and went so far as to demand it. They definitely attract the best and brightest to work for them in Cupertino, just outside San Francisco.

The former marketer and now venture capitalist Guy Kawasaki worked for Steve in the early days and was part of the Macintosh launch team. His experience of working for Jobs matches other accounts. In an interview with Dan Lyons of *ReadWrite* Kawasaki said that, despite his experience there being a huge challenge, working for Jobs 'was definitely the formative experience of my life'. Kawasaki described Jobs as 'truly a visionary', but said that he could be vicious. 'I lived in fear of being ripped and shredded in front of hundreds of people.'

I was in the Sydney Apple store last year running a series of seminars on public speaking and confess that I am a total Fan-Boy for Apple products — no apology. While speaking with the team of youngsters and geniuses, the topic of what it's like to work at Apple came up. Steve as tyrant, emotional intelligence training and the Think Different ad were all discussed. There was an extraordinary buzz and energy in the team regarding the ad. Most were not born when it aired, but nonetheless the message was one they identified with proudly some 20 years on. Talk about enduring amplification — could Jennifer and the team at Chiat/Day have had any idea of the impact their work was going to have on the culture of Apple?

The Think Different campaign by Apple actually built 29 different poster sets. The names and the obvious back stories read like an Amplifiers Hall of Fame list. These included the likes of Pablo Picasso, Mahatma Ghandi, Thomas Edison, Jim Henson, the Dalai Lama, Miles Davis and many more.

Reading the back-stories of each of these 29 amplifiers would be great follow-up inspiration for students of amplification. One year, in Cupertino, all the Apple staff were given a book with all the posters in them — gorgeous!

Too often we are scared

I have a dear friend, Dan Gregory. He is an adviser — a sounding board and a gun thought leader. As a modern-day 'Mad man' and creative director of some of our country's leading ad campaigns, I asked him to share one of his favourite pieces of pop literature or amplification. He chose a Nike ad. Here are the first two lines. It's worth a google to read the full piece.

> Too often we are scared.
> Scared of what we might not be able to do.

This piece calls you to action. It helps you identify with the heroic amplifier within. Nike has gone on to create a range of motivational ads and messages — definitely worth checking out. I have posted some, including the Find Your Greatness campaign ads, onto the *Amplifiers* website at www.amplifiersthebook.com.

Obama's hope

I'm not sure how history will remember the time Barack Obama has spent in the White House. At the time of writing this he is into his second term and still mired down by the divisive partisan politics that obstruct leadership effectiveness in a democracy. So make no mistake—I do realise that motivational leadership is simply a part of the game of effective change in people and families. You also need resources, a mandate and so much more to be an effective leader. My goal in writing this book is not to establish motivational leadership as the panacea to all that ails the world. I am saying that it is a critical piece of the puzzle. I may even go so far as to say it's the key to getting things started.

The speech Barack Obama gave the night we got news he was the first African American to be elected president went viral around the world. Where were you when you first watched it? Embedded in this transcript I have added some comments as headings. These are context summaries of the paragraph that follows. You can see the flow of the message through these words alone. The whole speech is built around the overarching context of 'Hope! A change we can believe in'.

Significance

If there is anyone out there who still doubts that America is a place where all things are possible; who still wonders if the dream of our founders is alive in our time; who still questions the power of our democracy, tonight is your answer card.

It's the answer told by lines that stretched around schools and churches in numbers this nation has never seen; by people who waited three hours and four hours, many for the very first time in their lives, because they believed that this time must be different; that their voice could be that difference.

Diversity

It's the answer spoken by young and old, rich and poor, Democrat and Republican, black, white, Latino, Asian, Native American, gay, straight, disabled and not disabled—Americans who sent a message to the world that we have never been a collection of Red States and Blue States: we are, and always will be, the United States of America.

Hope

It's the answer that led those who have been told for so long by so many to be cynical, and fearful, and doubtful of what we can achieve to put their hands on the arc of history and bend it once more toward the hope of a better day.

Significance (2)

It's been a long time coming, but tonight, because of what we did on this day, in this election, at this defining moment, change has come to America.

Respect

I just received a very gracious call from Senator McCain. He fought long and hard in this campaign, and he's fought even longer and harder for the country he loves. He has endured sacrifices for America that most of us cannot begin to imagine, and we are better off for the service rendered by this brave and selfless leader. I congratulate him and Governor Palin for all they have achieved, and I look forward to working with them to renew this nation's promise in the months ahead.

Gratitude

I want to thank my partner in this journey, a man who campaigned from his heart and spoke for the men and women he grew up with on the streets of Scranton and rode with on that train home to Delaware, the Vice President-elect of the United States, Joe Biden.

I would not be standing here tonight without the unyielding support of my best friend for the last sixteen years, the rock of our family and the love of my life, our nation's next First Lady, Michelle Obama. Sasha and Malia, I love you both so much, and you have earned the new puppy that's coming with us to the White House. And while she's no longer with us, I know my grandmother is watching, along with the family that made me who I am. I miss them tonight, and know that my debt to them is beyond measure.

To my campaign manager David Plouffe, my chief strategist David Axelrod, and the best campaign team ever assembled in the history of politics — you made this happen, and I am forever grateful for what you've sacrificed to get it done.

Humility

But above all, I will never forget who this victory truly belongs to — it belongs to you.

I was never the likeliest candidate for this office. We didn't start with much money or many endorsements. Our campaign was not hatched in the halls of Washington — it began in the backyards of Des Moines and the living rooms of Concord and the front porches of Charleston.

Service

It was built by working men and women who dug into what little savings they had to give five dollars and ten dollars and twenty dollars to this cause. It grew strength from the young people who rejected the myth of their generation's apathy; who left their homes and their families for jobs that offered little pay and less sleep; from the not-so-young people who braved the bitter cold and scorching heat to knock on the doors of perfect strangers; from the millions of Americans who volunteered, and organized, and proved that more than two centuries later, a government of the people, by the people and for the people has not perished from this Earth. This is your victory.

I know you didn't do this just to win an election and I know you didn't do it for me. You did it because you understand the enormity of the task that lies ahead. For even as we celebrate tonight, we know the challenges that tomorrow will bring are the greatest of our lifetime—two wars, a planet in peril, the worst financial crisis in a century. Even as we stand here tonight, we know there are brave Americans waking up in the deserts of Iraq and the mountains of Afghanistan to risk their lives for us. There are mothers and fathers who will lie awake after their children fall asleep and wonder how they'll make the mortgage, or pay their doctor's bills, or save enough for college. There is new energy to harness and new jobs to be created; new schools to build and threats to meet and alliances to repair.

Expectations

The road ahead will be long. Our climb will be steep. We may not get there in one year or even one term, but America—I have never been more hopeful than I am tonight that we will get there. I promise you—we as a people will get there.

There will be setbacks and false starts. There are many who won't agree with every decision or policy I make as President, and we know that government can't solve every problem. But I will always be honest with you about the challenges we face. I will listen to you, especially when we disagree. And above all, I will ask you to join in the work of remaking this nation the only way it's been done in America for two-hundred and twenty-one years—block by block, brick by brick, calloused hand by calloused hand.

Perseverance

What began twenty-one months ago in the depths of winter must not end on this autumn night. This victory alone is not the change we seek—it is only the chance for us to make that change. And that cannot happen if we go back to the way things were. It cannot happen without you.

Responsibility

So let us summon a new spirit of patriotism; of service and responsibility where each of us resolves to pitch in and work harder and look after not only ourselves, but each other. Let us remember that if this financial crisis taught us anything, it's that we cannot have a thriving Wall Street while Main Street suffers—in this country, we rise or fall as one nation; as one people.

Local unity

Let us resist the temptation to fall back on the same partisanship and pettiness and immaturity that has poisoned our politics for so long. Let us remember that it was a man from this state who first carried the banner of the Republican Party to the White House—a party founded on the values of self-reliance, individual liberty, and national unity. Those are values we all share, and while the Democratic Party has won a great victory tonight, we do so with a measure of humility and determination to heal the divides that have held back our progress. As Lincoln said to a nation far more divided than ours, 'We are not enemies, but friends…though passion may have strained it must not break our bonds of affection.' And to those Americans whose support I have yet to earn—I may not have won your vote, but I hear your voices, I need your help, and I will be your President too.

Global unity

And to all those watching tonight from beyond our shores, from parliaments and palaces to those who are huddled around radios in the forgotten corners of our world—our stories are singular, but our destiny is shared, and a new dawn of American leadership is at hand. To those who would tear this world down—we will defeat you. To those who seek peace and security—we support you. And to all those who have wondered if America's beacon still burns as bright—tonight we proved once more that the true strength of our nation comes not from the might of our arms or the scale of our wealth, but from the enduring power of our ideals: democracy, liberty, opportunity, and unyielding hope.

Pride

For that is the true genius of America—that America can change. Our union can be perfected. And what we have already achieved gives us hope for what we can and must achieve tomorrow.

Personalisation

This election had many firsts and many stories that will be told for generations. But one that's on my mind tonight is about a woman who cast her ballot in Atlanta. She's a lot like the millions of others who stood in line to make their voice heard in this election except for one thing—Ann Nixon Cooper is 106 years old.

She was born just a generation past slavery; a time when there were no cars on the road or planes in the sky; when someone like her couldn't vote for two reasons—because she was a woman and because of the color of her skin.

Momentous moments (linked to Personalisation)

And tonight, I think about all that she's seen throughout her century in America—the heartache and the hope; the struggle and the progress; the times we were told that we can't, and the people who pressed on with that American creed: Yes we can.

At a time when women's voices were silenced and their hopes dismissed, she lived to see them stand up and speak out and reach for the ballot. Yes we can.

When there was despair in the dust bowl and depression across the land, she saw a nation conquer fear itself with a New Deal, new jobs and a new sense of common purpose. Yes we can.

When the bombs fell on our harbor and tyranny threatened the world, she was there to witness a generation rise to greatness and a democracy was saved. Yes we can.

She was there for the buses in Montgomery, the hoses in Birmingham, a bridge in Selma, and a preacher from Atlanta who told a people that 'We Shall Overcome.' Yes we can.

A man touched down on the moon, a wall came down in Berlin, a world was connected by our own science and imagination. And this year, in this election, she touched her finger to a screen, and cast her vote, because after 106 years in America, through the best of times and the darkest of hours, she knows how America can change. Yes we can.

America, we have come so far. We have seen so much. But there is so much more to do. So tonight, let us ask ourselves—if our children should live to see the next century; if my daughters should be so lucky to live as long as Ann Nixon Cooper, what change will they see? What progress will we have made?

Inspiration

This is our chance to answer that call. This is our moment. This is our time—to put our people back to work and open doors of opportunity for our kids; to restore prosperity and promote the cause of peace; to reclaim the American Dream and reaffirm that fundamental truth—that out of many, we are one; that while we breathe, we hope, and where we are met with cynicism, and doubt, and those who tell us that we can't, we will respond with that timeless creed that sums up the spirit of a people:

Mantra

Yes We Can. Thank you, God bless you, and may God Bless the United States of America.

A perfect piece of amplification. Regardless of what you think of Obama in the White House, you have to acknowledge that one of the three main contributors to his success was his ability to connect with the mood of the times and inspire people to believe in his vision. No doubt his fundraising strategies contributed (through Facebook early stager Chris Hughes), as did the general disillusionment of the everyday American towards George W. Bush. And the fact that they were facing wars on several fronts and serious economic challenges at home all helped. But I don't believe he would be in the White House if he hadn't been able to inspire people to believe!

Eat, Pray, Love

I'm on vacation on a Pacific Island. The kids are swimming in the crystal clear blue water in front of me. I am working my way through my second capriosca for the day. My gorgeous wife, Lexie, through inspired tears, stops me reading a book with a significant body count and states with conviction, 'If you want to understand me you will stop what you are doing and read this!' At which point she hands me a copy of Elisabeth Gilbert's semi-autobiographical journey in the now famous *Eat Pray Love: One Woman's Search for Everything Across Italy, India and Indonesia*.

So I put down Andy McNab's latest and somewhat reluctantly start reading. Within minutes Gilbert has got me. Damn — I may have to actually read this one. Several hours later I put the book down, totally inspired by her powerful use of language. Gilbert maximises to both engage and inspire. A key to understanding amplification in action.

Elisabeth Gilbert's TED talk on the elusive nature of genius is an essay on the power of words to move and motivate. Here is a small piece of her TED talk. As you would expect, you can watch the full talk on the *Amplifiers* website at www.amplifiersthebook.com.

> O.K. Centuries ago in the deserts of North Africa, people used to gather for these moonlight dances of sacred dance and music that would go on for hours and hours, until dawn. And they were always magnificent, because the dancers were professionals and they were terrific, right? But every once in a while, very rarely, something would happen, and one of these performers would actually become transcendent…all of a sudden, he would no longer appear to be merely human. He would be lit from within, and lit from below and all lit up on fire with divinity.

Special thanks to the team at TED and the Sapling Foundation for making these extraordinary moments available free to all.

Word up!

In the communication world, an often-quoted (and frequently misquoted) study by communication researcher Albert Mehrabian describes how people communicate. Mehrabian and his colleagues were seeking to understand the relative impact of facial expressions, vocal tone and spoken words in communication. Most people conclude, based on the Mehrabian studies—that only 7 per cent of communication effectiveness is based on the words you choose. As a result, people then say that it's not what you say, it's how you say it that is important, and they tend to quote Mehrabian's study to prove their point. But they shouldn't; they are misquoting him to focus on technique over content. They are pushing a one-sided agenda based on at best incorrect assumptions and at worst a manipulation of data to draw a false conclusion. Words really do matter.

The misunderstanding

Mehrabian concluded that when people are in rapport, they begin to pay more attention to vocal tone and facial expressions than they do to the words.

This has been subsequently generalised to mean that in all communication:

- 7 per cent happens in spoken words.
- 38 per cent happens through voice tone.
- 55 per cent happens via general body language.

This is, of course, not true.

This generalisation twists the study to conveniently de-emphasise content, message and great words. I think that this is probably a ploy (maybe a subconscious one) to avoid coaching on content and message by people who teach communication skills, which is understandable. You have to pay more attention when working with what someone says, and you have to bring a level of intelligence and subject matter expertise to add value, lacking that all you have is technique. That doesn't make it right.

Some safe conclusions from Mehrabian's study may be:

- Communication is not just words—a lot of communication is non-verbal.

- Without seeing and hearing non-verbal communication, it is easier to misunderstand the words.

- When we are unsure and we trust the other person less, we pay more attention to the words being said.

Many families choose to remove the word 'hate' from their vocabulary. Similarly, many educators are taught to eliminate the pejorative *but* from their language. 'I love you *but*', effectively eliminates what was said before it. People hear nothing except what comes after the *but*. Choose words carefully and be intentional around the use of words.

Ignite the pejorative

Ash Bennet, a speaker and gay activist from Boulder, Colorado, is unknown to many. The focus of her message addresses a hurtful piece of language. This is one gay woman's intelligent declaration— rant if you will—about the importance of what you say and the unintentional impact of our words.

Ash invites us all to realise that words matter and that we should never be casual about our word choice. Ash is an amplifier, and her message is worth reading and watching. The video is on the *Amplifier* website.

My name is Ash and I can say unequivocally that I am so gay.

My Ignite topic is eliminating the word gay as a pejorative from our lexicon.

I'll explain to you the difference between what I just said and what this image conveys.

Now you may be saying: 'Ash we live in Boulder, we love gays here'.

We have Pride, we have BCAP [Boulder County AIDS Project]. All true.

But I guarantee you there are places you go everyday where someone will describe something pejoratively as 'so gay' despite the fact that it's neither homosexual nor happy.

Now why is this important?

First of all it's critical to know that there is a difference between tolerance and acceptance. Tolerance is 'to put up with', 'the capacity to endure continued subjection to something'. Now I don't know about you, but that is not exactly something I strive for.

Acceptance, on the other hand is 'to regard as proper, normal, or inevitable'—'To recognize to be true'. Tolerance is when the school district *allows* you to bring your same sex date to the prom. Acceptance is when your classmates don't whisper and laugh when you dance. The difference is tremendous. Now, 'gay' is not the first word in our language that needs a makeover. All of these words evoke emotion.

They are hard to read, hard to say.

Your body physically reacts to seeing these words. I have a similar reaction when I hear somebody describe something pejoratively as 'so gay'.

I was at a gym in Boulder once and a trainer was teaching us how to spot and another trainer came up and said 'well you better never grab me like that dude, that's so gay'.

And he was just saying that to give his buddy a hard time.

But can you hear the homophobia in it?

Now there's plenty of things it's okay to call gay:

Me—for example. [Showing a slide of people and characters she says] The top row: they've all come out. Now the bottom row?

...we cross our fingers but until they do...

They're cartoons and Muppets, so at the very least they're happy.

Now there's a long list of things that you should never call 'so gay'.

An assignment you don't want to do is not 'so gay'. Someone's new haircut is not 'so gay'.

A workout you hate is not 'so gay'.

A test that you bombed is not 'so gay'. Someone's car is not 'so gay'.

Now again, I may be preaching to the Boulder gay loving choir.

Some of you are gay.

Even more of you have gay friends.

But I chose this topic because you can legislate tolerance—you can't legislate acceptance.

That takes a societal shift.

So…so you're not sure if you should use the word 'gay'? Here's a flow chart. Is it a person? No.

Tough start—we'll get you on the next slide. So it is a person. Is it actually a self-identified homosexual? No? Are you describing their happiness?

Really their happiness? Then you're okay.

Alright, so it's not a person? Is a place or thing related to gay culture like a gay bar, or pride or a rainbow flag? Okay then you're good. If not, 'gay' is not the right word for you.

You're using it in a derogatory way.

What it often comes down to is not hate or bigotry but laziness. 'Gay' is a really easy word to throw in, but it's not what you're trying to convey.

Look at all these other options.

Say what you mean and mean what you say because the words that you choose matter.

When you use 'gay' in a pejorative way, the effect that it has on the gay kid in the room or the kid with gay relatives, is that being gay is less than, or inferior to. And our bar cannot be that a day that you just get through life—or just get to school, and don't get harassed—qualifies as a good day.

Now, in Boulder, we're much more like the guy on the right than the guy on the left.

Without question.

In Boulder, it's rarely so overt. But it does happen.

So when it does, what do you do?

What do you say to the trainer at the gym?

Do you just stomp out and quit your membership the next day? Do you muster your best Gary Coleman and just glare?

Or do you sit them down afterwards and say: 'hey you know what? I know you're just trying to dig your buddy but what you said was hurtful'.

That part's up to you.

You do what you can. No more—but certainly no less.

We need all hands in on this one.

Societal change begins with small steps.

When you hear someone describe something pejoratively as 'so gay', it's an opportunity for connection and conversation not to be missed. And silence is consent.

And you know what? We're better than that. We're Boulder—damn it.

And you all? You are the difference makers. You are parents and teachers and business owners and all in all just freaking awesome people, that have more influence than you give yourself credit for.

It speaks volumes in our society that we're more comfortable seeing a picture of two men holding guns than two men holding hands.

And the way that we right that is to make sure that the words that we use to describe the latter are never used in a way that is less than or demeaning or inferior to.

Now… I'm not perfect and I'm not trying to get you all to join the gay police.

I did this topic because I didn't have an answer for the guy at the gym.

I did my best Gary Coleman, but that was about it.

But, it inspired this. Talking to eight hundred and fifty people, instead of one.

So when you can: say *something*.

Because in the end, it takes a village, people.

I can't think of a better group of folks to make change happen than the people in this room. Thank you to Ignite for allowing me to speak.

And for those of you… and to those of you inspired to be part of the change, I thank you in advance for being the change you wish to seek. Enjoy the rest of your night.

I love it! What a fabulous piece of amplification in action: see, it's not just talk.

The interesting thing about Ash's talk is the reactions it's creating. Like all things viral, the emotional responses are wide and varied. Tolerance is not acceptance.

Words are magical

The late David Hawkins, a kinesiology educator and author, is considered by many to be either a pariah or a prophet. Regardless of the story behind who he is, what he did or whether you should care—he advanced some brilliant thinking on the power of words.

The background is a bit 'woo hoo', but a book on amplifiers probably needs a bit of 'woo hoo' to make it less 'blah blah' anyway. The right words delivered at the right moment tune the room. Just as poetry and music call us to be our best self at times, you may say we are operating at higher, constructive evolutionary frequencies when talking about love than we are when living in hate.

This is the idea of picking up on and managing the energy in a room when things go wrong because of a certain frequency of ideas. Some ideas kind of resonate at a higher level of consciousness than others. Let's assume positive ideas resonate higher than negative.

Table 11.1 (overleaf) illustrates the idea of frequencies and a word ladder of sorts from concepts that are lower in their vibration up to concepts and words that are higher. To put this together, I have meshed together the thinking of Don Beck and Clare Graves, values and behaviour experts, with *Spiral Dynamics* and David Hawkins's *Power vs Force*. I also drew on the work of my dear friends Michael and Shah Henderson, anthropologists and authors, in their book *Leading Through Values*, and in particular their work on world views. You can search their work on the internet, or buy books on values in a good management/leadership book store. The basic premise I am drawing from the collective works referenced above is that ideas/moods exist on a logarithmic scale. More baseline feelings, such as anger and hate, are lower than compassion and joy.

The idea that feelings and moods operate in a hierarchy is a fascinating concept in its own right and is well worth the time to learn more. In the context of speaking, though, it's pretty simple. If a room is exhibiting a predominant mood, say of anger, as an amplifier you should meet the anger, and then lift the tone by one level, to turn the frequency up a notch. Essentially you respond to the mood that is (don't react), you then elevate the mood by discussing the ideas one level up from the prevailing. In this way words and ideas being to shift the inner dialogue.

Table 11.1 (overleaf) shows the hierarchy of ideas in a word ladder. I believe amplifiers should study this ladder and get good at recognising, responding to and elevating the frequency of conversation.

Table 11.1: word ladder

Message	Language	Process
Peace	We are all connected.	Increase awareness.
Meaning	It all makes sense.	Establish context.
Hope	There is another way.	Inspire belief.
Courage	You can do it.	Empower to act.
Pride	We are the best.	Inflate position.
Expectations	You can do better.	Share disappointment
Fear	Be afraid of what is to come.	Withdraw support.
Blame	It's all your fault.	Destroy relationships.

Here are some ideas about ways to shift the mood, turn up the frequency and harness the power of words.

- Name the prevailing mood. Using the feel/felt/found approach is a good way to approach this. 'I understand how you may be feeling [name the emotion or mood]. I have felt the same when [recall time], but I have found that [insert reframe or preferred state or outcome].'

- Weave the mood into a story that expresses a mood one notch above the prevailing mood, and concludes several levels above where you started. This can get people to see that you understand where they are at, and still lifts up the mood.

- Ask courageous questions. Ask questions around what it would take to be courageous, and see the challenge before the audience in a different and constructive fashion. David Hawkins's book, *Power Vs. Force*, unpacks courage as the key turning point in moving from defensive negative patterns of thought and dialogue to more positive ones.

At a glance

Tune in to the mood in the room. People process information through different channels. Know the channels that you prefer, and develop capabilities in those channels for which you don't have such a preference.

Get paranoid. A lot of the negative stuff that happens in a room when people speak could have been fixed with a little bit of planning. Manage the problems that you believe may arise when you are speaking, based on who you are, what you are talking about, or to whom you are speaking.

Don't let the turkeys get you down. Argument and disagreement occur in territorial disputes around content. Stay clean on your context and you can avoid much of the hostility and anger you may otherwise get. Things get messy when you dip into people's content. You end up either having to accept or reject their truth and experience, an act that typically doesn't end well.

Lift the room. Know the idea ladder and get a feel for the prevailing mood of the room. Pitch your speech at a level they understand, and at the same time, at a level they want. Focus on the high-order, 'above the line' emotions and themes.

Blood sweat and tears

Most leadership books tell of organisations that stand out because of their focus on cost control (Toyota), their innovative product development (Apple) or possibly their extreme customer service (Zappos), and while the business profiled in this chapter is a worthy business to study, it is the motivational leadership that makes it rock. What is also remarkable about this business is the fact that it has a decentralised motivational leadership model. Make no mistake, there is plenty of rah-rah at the top of the organisation, but it's actually the total business embracing of motivational leadership that sets it apart.

It's rumoured, but it has never been proven, that Winston Churchill once said, 'Whenever I get the urge to exercise, I lie down and it passes'. If you, like Churchill, would rather beat your head against a wall than exercise, this business will be an unknown to you. If, however, you have wandered into a gym somewhere in the world, you are likely to be familiar with the name Les Mills, or at the very least the company's star product, BODYPUMP. Les Mills International (LMI) is named after the entrepreneurial ex-mayor of Auckland, New Zealand, Les Mills. He was a famous athlete who represented New Zealand at the Olympics and Commonwealth Games for more than two decades. He was a powerful and popular man and certainly one who had command of the skill of amplification. The Les Mills franchise is now a global business with some staggering success metrics. Our story, though rooted in his influence, really takes off in the 1990s when his son Phillip focused on taking Les Mills group exercise to the world and subsequently grew the business to extraordinary heights.

Starting its life as bricks and mortar fitness centres distributed throughout New Zealand, the business brand for many years remained simply a chain of fitness clubs. The fitness centre business model has always been a tough one to monetise. It's a challenging game because the product requires some personal discipline in the mind of your customer. It's easy to sell someone on joining a gym. It's hard to get them to turn up and use the product. While health and fitness at a superficial level is all about the body, the actual game is won or lost in the mind of your customer. At it's most basic level the business is about helping people overcome inertia and apathy, and go on a transformational journey of self-discipline, commitment and often pain. Sounds like a job for motivational leadership.

It was when Phillip, the son of Les Mills, and his celebrity doctor wife, Jackie, began to run the business that it began to take on something magical—a quality of culture that makes it a giant among businesses today and a model worth studying and emulating.

The DNA of the magic in this business was clear even in the early days. Instructors of the LMI brand had a certain swagger. I clearly remember attending the World Aerobics Championships and seeing three-times world champion Brett Fairweather perform extraordinary feats of athleticism while dressed as Fred Flintstone. It was staggeringly entertaining and at the same time undeniably skilful.

I remember exploring the success of this business in a sleepy town in New Zealand called Hamilton. I watched, stunned, while two powerful Maori men led 250 everyday gym members through what I can only now call an 'experience'. It was no mere workout. What makes this remarkable is that it was 7 am on Sunday morning! In any other group exercise environment you would be lucky if 12 people turned up.

It was many years later when working with Steve Renata, one of the founding figures in the business, that I started to understand what was going one. For international readers, it's worth pausing for a moment to explain that I am a white Australian and have no right to comment on the powerful Maori race of New Zealand. I do so with respect and only an observer's knowledge. Steve is a charismatic Maori leader. He walks into a room and many swoon. It's always been this way. I have known Steve for more than 15 years and as he ages this effect only seems to get worse.

Steve carries what the Maori call *mana*. It's a force, a way of being. It's less about words and more about carriage. Call it 'swagger', call it charisma. It is powerful and has huge commercial leadership benefits. Trying to understand where this came from I began to study from a distance the culture of both the Maori and the LMI business.

I was truly fortunate one year to be the guest speaker at one of LMI's annual global summits, which was held in New Zealand, for the top leaders in the LMI business, and what I saw has never been repeated, not even close, at any other corporate gathering of global leaders. It doesn't help that the leaders are all super fit, genetically gifted body-gods. Add to that that most hold a bachelor's or master's degree in biomechanics, education, sports medicine or some related applied science, and you have a potent mix. So they are smart, fit and full of energy.

All this talent is not unique to LMI. Many who make it their mission to help others to stay well hold the same qualifications and outstanding commitment to wellness. What differentiated the LMI tribe is exactly that — they are a tribe — quite literally. I saw strapping blond Swedish men and women, total stereotypes, with one fundamental difference. Many sported the Maori half sleeve arm tattoo, circumnavigating the biceps. What drives a proud Swede to wear the markings of a small island tribe in the Southern Hemisphere? It floored me, and I don't mind admitting I was a little intimidated. You see, I was the opening speaker—the motivational speaker. It felt like any one of them should take the stage instead of me. I was going to have to dig deep if I was going to rock this room.

They were sold on, and indeed committed to, the LMI culture because of the inherent power of motivational leadership, amplification, to make a difference—and I was the opening speaker. In my mind I was thinking, 'Game on, time to bring it Churchie'. To make matters worse, the conference didn't start like most do. I should have known I was not in Kansas any more when—instead of an opening address—the agenda listed the slot before I went on as the opening ceremony. No joke—there was dry ice, thumping music, emotional videos and some serious crowd engagement. And to make matters worse, all that was happening before the event even started!

I would normally write that the 2800 attendees shuffled into the conference hall. It would be more accurate to say these 2800 people erupted into the room. Most nations and all continents of the planet were represented, the lion share of delegates having travelled on international carriers for more than 24 hours the day before just to be in the founding home of this global business. They were chanting their country of origin, and no joke, I saw audience members walking in on their hands—some performing cartwheels and back flips as they took their chairs. Put yourself in my position—I was their motivational speaker for the day—gulp. It was as if I had stumbled into some weird alternative universe.

The Maori *haka* is a thing to behold. If you are a rugby union fan you will recognise it as a fierce dance of sorts conducted by the All Blacks rugby team before any match of significance.

In 1996 the Australian rugby team, the Wallabies, upset many New Zealanders when before the Wellington Test, they decided to turn their backs on the *haka*, warming up at the other end of Athletic Park instead. The tactic, which did not have the full support of the Australian players that day but was driven by team management, didn't work as the Wallabies suffered their biggest loss to the All Blacks—a 43-6 thrashing.

Ignorance of the purpose and power of the *haka* allowed this abhorrent behaviour. It's easy to interpret the *haka* as an attempt to intimidate—the warlike movements and fierce facial expressions make it easy to confuse the intent. To the Maori, the *haka* is a call to ferocity—a signal that what is about to happen could be truly magnificent. It's an invitation to the opponent to bring it on, hold nothing back, and play magnificently! To turn your back on this invitation is to miss the point all together. As an Australian my ignorance was remedied by this international sporting incident.

I will never forget what I witnessed before going on stage that morning. I saw a Maori tribal leader present Phillip Mills, a white man, with a feather cloak, known as a *kahu huruhuru* recognising his position as the chief of the tribe. This was followed by the sharing of breath, known as a *hongi*. This was an essential part of the opening ceremony as local Maori leaders went on to gift the LMI business with their very own *haka*, something never before done for a commercial organisation. It was a very moving event.

My friend Steve took some time to explain what was happening that morning, just before I went on to speak. The LMI organisation, a money-making business, was about to be the first commercial enterprise to have a custom-built *haka* choreographed and gifted to them, something that is unlikely to be repeated anywhere else again. A powerful dance ritual that celebrated the human form, the *haka* was beautiful to behold and something that invoked a tribal roar from the gathering. Here are the words of the *haka* in Maori with an English translation alongside.

Tu Mai Nei Nga Toa E	Les Mills Haka
Kaitataki: Kia wiri Hope Ki raro A kia mau Hi Kia whakata hoki au i ahau Hi Aue Hi E nga matua tipuna tukua mai te kaha te rangatiratanga e	Leader: Let your hands quiver by your side Hands on hips, Hands down by your side (still) Be steadfast Let me be at one with the earth Hi aue hi Ancient ancestors/warriors of old bestow upon us strength and leadership
Kapa: Tu mai nei nga toa e Haka ana ki te noho mangere Ko te whakaara ko te momona Me pakanga, parekura e Kia pakari hinengaro, tinana, wairua. Ko te ha o tane e	Group: Standing here are the new warriors We haka in fury at sedentary lifestyles Obesity is our adversary Let us do battle Let your mind, body and spiritual essence be revitalised Through the breath of life
Kaitataki: I te wehenga ka puta hihiri e	Leader: At the separation of earth from sky, all potential was released into this world
Kapa: Na reira, me puta to ihi e Kia tu te wana Kia tu te wero aue Kia tu kotahi tatou Ana, Ana, Ana, Tenei whakatau. Hi.	Group: Therefore, let your true potential be known Reveal your inner strength and power Hold fast to the challenge Let us unite as one global entity Yes it is , Yes it is, Yes it is This we decree.

Now, just after this powerful moment, I hear a voice from the distance, announcing the next speaker. Seriously, who wants to follow that? I hear the words 'Ladies and Gentleman, to open our event today please give a huge LMI welcome to Maaaaatttttt Church!' Seriously, what do you say after that? My inner voice starts nattering away 'Open it, come on, it is already split wide open. I don't think PowerPoint slides will be enough today!'

As I reflect on my experience with the LMI crew I reckon there are five lessons for amplifiers that are worth noting:

- *Strategy and culture are a potent mix.* Motivational leadership is the bridge that deploys them in parallel.

- *Big audacious missions and reasons-for-being glue people together.* They give people something to aim for, regardless of results.

- *Motivational leadership needs to be decentralised and not held at the top of an organisation.* A message that motivates from peers — not the boss — is 10 times more motivating.

- *Experiences trump memos.* Don't tell people how you want them to be. Create environments that allow them to be more than that.

- *Resources are less important than people.* Innovation, expansion and market domination can be achieved with less money than you think — if the business is led by spirited people.

Final words

Thank you for coming on this journey. I hope to have played a small part in paying forward the idea that not only do leaders matter, but they also make a difference. They do so by amplifying the good. Everyone can lead — it's a choice not a position. Amplification is what you do.

So why not join the evolution? It's an evolution, not a revolution; it's a gentle acceptance of the maturity of motivation done right. It's not a revolutionary idea or a 180-degree about-face in direction or action. To be an amplifier is to work with what is and make the most of it, not to reject what is or try to replace it with something new.

We have created an elegant little logo that we send to people who choose to join the Amplifier Evolution. To get it you simply go to the Amplifiers website, sign the pledge and we send you the logo. Put it on your social media platforms; place it in a résumé or simply go through the process of committing to amplification, committing to being a difference maker.

We also offer poster packs and facilitator guides to help you implement a culture of amplification in and around you.

Written with love, light and hope: let that be your predominant experience and activity from this point forward.

Index

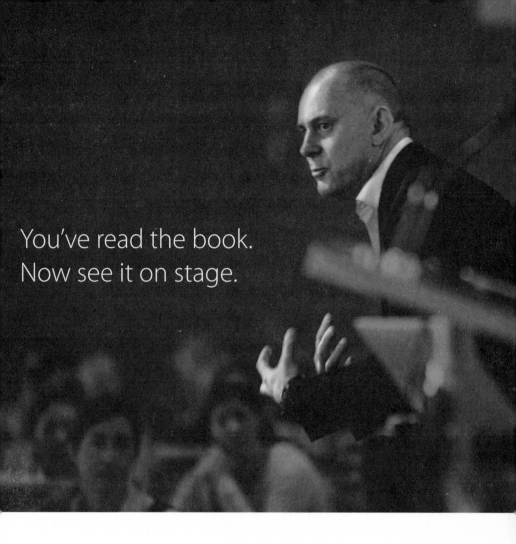

You've read the book.
Now see it on stage.

Matt Church understands like few others that organisations
which succeed have leaders who are inspired by what they
do and what their work stands for.

He has a rare ability to bring a room full of people along
with him for this ride. Matt's highly informative, humorous and
energetic style saw him awarded the 2014—15 Australian
Speaker of the Year, and he was recently named one of the
Top 10 motivational speakers in the world.

So find out how he can inspire your organisation: in a theatre
before thousands or a boardroom with just your key leaders.

mattchurch.com

Helping clever people
become commercially smart

BUSINESS
SCHOOL

Matt Church has long been passionate about helping experts deepen their thinking, broaden their reach, and increase their impact. Thought Leaders Business School is the culmination of over twenty years of his ideas and experience.

So if you have an idea you need to share with the world, Matt and the Business School team can dramatically expand your capacity to make an impact and be rewarded for it.

tlbusinessschool.com

Learn more with practical advice from our experts

Digilogue
Anders Sörman-Nilsson

The New Rules of Management
Peter Cook

Stop Playing Safe
Margie Warrell

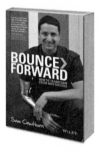

Bounce Forward
Sam Cawthorn

The One Thing to Win At the Game of Business
Creel Price

The People Manager's Toolkit
Karen Gately

Play a Bigger Game
Rowdy McLean

Hooked
Gabrielle Dolan and Yamini Naidu

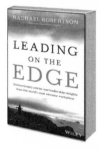

Leading on the Edge
Rachael Robertson